Because I Don't Have Wings

Because I Don't Have Wings
Stories of Mexican Immigrant Life

PHILIP GARRISON

THE UNIVERSITY OF ARIZONA PRESS

Tucson

This is a work of creative nonfiction. With the exception of Jim Bodeen, the individuals portrayed are composites created by combining features of real people, protecting their privacy without changing the spirit of the story. Resemblances to persons living or dead owe to the spirit of the story or to coincidence.

The University of Arizona Press
© 2006 Philip Garrison
⊗ This book is printed on acid-free, archival-quality paper.
Manufactured in the United States of America

11   10   09   08   07   06   6   5   4   3   2   1

Library of Congress Cataloging-in-Publication Data

Garrison, Philip.
  Because I don't have wings : stories of Mexican immigrant life / Philip Garrison.
    p. cm.
Includes bibliographical references (p.).
ISBN-13: 978-0-8165-2525-6 (pbk. : alk. paper)
ISBN-10: 0-8165-2525-0 (pbk. : alk. paper)
1. Mexicans—Inland Empire—Social life and customs—Anecdotes. 2. Immigrants—Inland Empire—Social life and customs—Anecdotes. 3. Community life—Inland Empire—Anecdotes. 4. Inland Empire—Social life and customs—Anecdotes. 5. Inland Empire—Ethnic relations—Anecdotes. 6. Mexicans—Inland Empire—Languages. 7. Figures of speech. 8. Inland Empire—Emigration and immigration. 9. Michoacán de Ocampo (Mexico)—Emigration and immigration. I. Title.
F855.2.M5G37 2006
305.868'7207237–dc22

                                        2005024585

Publication of this book is made possible in part by the proceeds of a permanent endowment created with the assistance of a Challenge Grant from the National Endowment for the Humanities, a federal agency.

for Patricia

CONTENTS

PREFACE: LA RECONQUISTA

This is a book about the Third World and the First, about their making contact in an isolated niche of the United States, the Inland Northwest. Set at the end of a century in which the government made deserts bloom, it examines a huge, ungainly, and largely illegal guest worker program. How did such a program come into being? Dams in the U.S. West created conditions in which migrant laborers, needing to migrate fewer miles, began to live year-round in one of the valleys that wrinkle the West between the Cascades and the Rockies, valleys like the one I live in.

As a "border book," this one shares the interest of Davidson's *Lives on the Line,* Taylor and Hickey's *Tunnel Kids,* and Urrea's *Lake of Sleeping Children.* Except that their books are set on the border proper, while I report from 1,500 miles north of the "official" international boundary. Unlike Rubén Martínez's marvelous *Crossing Over,* which follows several indigenous Purépecha families from Michoacán to work they find in St. Louis and farther north, this book features an ad hoc community, a loose collection of families from Michoacán and surrounding states, mestizos settled a scant 150 miles south of the Canadian line.

My neighbors are so far from home that adaptation sprouts all over them, and hardens into a kind of exile. Made of offhand remarks and family spats and plain gossip, the horizons here are those of a stationary, loose-knit community three days' drive north of Tijuana. We're five days north of my neighbors' birthplaces in Michoacán, Jalisco, Guerrero, and Guanajuato.

Behind local orchards and hayfields, freeways and high-tension lines, the land is basin and range country. It wears stretch marks from lava flow and windy dust. One particular wall of floodwater, 2,000 feet high, with 500 cubic miles of lake behind it, cut scablands that resemble the surface of Mars. Aside from crops, local soil yields petrified tropical tree trunks, and fossilized horses and camels.

Lying between Wenatchee and Yakima—towns just as distant from the border, but which have attracted Mexican agricultural labor since the Bracero Program of the 1940s—my community dates from only ten or fifteen years ago, when the first families arrived. The community's founding is recent enough to make it a kind of time capsule, one where immigrants still are getting used to Anglos and to each other, an earlier stage of that "pioneer" process that has turned Latinos into the West Coast's largest ethnic minority.

Its rapid rate of turnover—a constant in any boomtown—multiplies my community's isolation. The severity of the winters and the seasonal nature of most employment make the annual rate of replacement something like thirty percent. Neighborhoods form and dissolve and form again. Family members who leave stay in touch, more or less, but friends vanish so fast all you recall is a nickname. No market or plaza exists for people to gather at. They meet at weddings and christenings, *quinceañera* gatherings and funerals, as well as at the food bank that two friends and I started ten years ago.

And my own perspective on all this? A lot of it owes to my being a writer, a person given to listening and describing. The rest of it owes to what is, apparently, my default setting in some inner program—by which I mean that as an adult I discovered that I "spoke Spanish." While I was in school, I studied languages—Latin, Russian, French—dutifully, but with no interest. I went through grammar drills and earned degrees at English-speaking, midwestern universities. In 1965, because an opening existed there, I entered the academic workforce in El Paso, Texas. But the first time I crossed that downtown bridge into the other world that mid-sixties Ciudad Juárez was, it felt like meeting a version of myself I didn't know existed: I could read the billboards. I understood what people on the sidewalk said to each other, more or less. I couldn't get enough of the place!

I knew at the time it didn't make sense. What was happening in my head? Born to parents from Missouri, to grandparents from Oklahoma, Minnesota, Ireland even, where would I have heard Spanish spoken enough that suddenly, as a young adult, I knew how to pronounce words, and to form simple sentences? Whatever was happening, I recall, it felt more like remembering than learning. But even now I can't explain it.

Not that I suffered any "identity crisis"—only a curiosity that, in time, shriveled. Who, after all, I asked myself, can account for love— or, in this case, belonging—at first sight? Like my family and friends, I've adapted by now to my "Mexican vanishing point." I think of it as a birthmark, a homely little enigma resistant over the years to any speculation this side of reincarnation.

There's more to the story, of course. But even now—after years of teaching assignments rotated between the Mexican Central Plateau and the U.S. Inland Northwest—especially when I feel more at ease in the guarded elaborations of Spanish than I do in English, it isn't a feeling I trace to any childhood source. It took getting used to, I admit. I crave the company of people from Mexico's Central Plateau. But, asked to account for that craving, my words wiggle off into pat answers, half-truths, pretexts.

Take how I met doña Carmen, my neighbor, who wears a single iron-colored braid between her shoulder blades. Slightly round-shouldered, with angular face and ample belly, born in the Jalisco hills, Carmen is all vigilance. Her ears and eyes miss nothing. The day we met in the food bank, eight years ago, when she wanted help filling out a form in English, I began to examine it—until her eyebrows stopped me.

"A ver," she wanted to know, "¿cómo será que Ud. habla como nosotros?" Not so fast—she wanted to know—how come I was talking like a Mexican? I looked her right in the eye. Pretext, I could tell, was everything. I said my grandmother came from Chihuahua.

Carmen thought it over. "Chihuahua, pues, Chihuahua es parte de México, ¿no?" Chihuahua was part of Mexico, Carmen was pretty sure. And I agreed. Whereupon she lifted both palms, both eyebrows went up—"¡pues por eso!"—to indicate that she and I together had figured out how come I talk like a Mexican.

The freewheeling pretexts of immigrant life! They are, alas, exactly what eludes the attention of U.S. mass media. Moments like that one with Carmen fly right by a mind-set predisposed to see people like Carmen as huddled masses a twenty-first-century United States dares not take to its bosom. Coverage lingers on the poor who inhabit border-town garbage dumps, or the rigors of the trip north, the sprinting and skulking, the helicopter spotlight playing on grass fanned flat. And all of that comes into play of course, but mixed with other moments—stubborn, intimate, truly unfilmable moments.

ACKNOWLEDGMENTS

Many thanks to the editors of the following journals, where earlier versions of some of these pieces appeared: *Fourth Genre* for "*Corrido*"; *North American Review* for "Postcards from Michoacán" (formerly "Nobody's Case Study"); *Northwest Review* for "Chain Letter" (formerly "The Last Nuance," named one of 100 notable essays of 1999 in *Best American Essays*, 2000), "Don Diego's Book" (formerly "I See These Things and Keep Quiet," named one of 100 notable essays of 2001 in *Best American Essays*, 2002), "Portraits from the Inland Empire" (formerly "Love Stories, Exile, and the Greek-Chorus Effect," named one of 100 notable essays of 1999 in *Best American Essays*, 2000), and "Patron Saint and Poster Boy" (formerly "Miracles, Possessions"); *Southwest Review* for "*Las Relaciones*" (formerly "La Reconquista in the Inland Empire," reprinted and translated into Spanish in *Tameme*); *Witness* for "Wets" (formerly "Working Wet").

My thanks go as well to colleagues on the 1993–94 Professional Leave Committee of Central Washington University.

Underlying a lot of what's written here is the thinking of two remarkable friends: Bill Dunning and José Licano Palma, *que descansen en paz.*

Lógico es que por fin las deudas más enredadas se pagan de la misma moneda. Así que por el apoyo y la amistad doy las gracias a las familias Calderón Bedolla, Carreón Calderón, Hernández Chávez, Hernández Flores, Nájar Aguilar, Nájar Suárez, y Sánchez Montoya.

I   La Reconquista

1 *Las Relaciones*

At arm's length, from the perspective of a relief globe, the area in question looks like a welt descending the western third of North America. Rockies to the east, and to the west the Cascade/Sierra Nevada range, these twin mountain chains isolate and intensify life down through Canada, then the United States. They acquire a single name, arriving at the Mexican border, Sierra Madre—Oriental, Occidental.

For a couple of hundred years, building railroads, following crops, Spanish-speaking people crossed the U.S.–Mexico border, wherever it happened to be. By the 1980s, some authorities thought the flow had doubled. Anglos living in counties their pioneer great-grandparents had named for politicians, or Indian nations, complained that where they lived had been invaded overnight. The 1980s yielded the classic story of the illegal alien apprehended by the *migra*, the INS. "Hey messican, how come you took off running?" the agent leered through the van's protective screen. "Por alas no tener," replied our man. Because I don't have wings.

That remark could be the motto of any number of señoras, in the Laundromat or supermarket aisle, chatting about children or weather, telephone deposit or parking ticket. It all leaks out in asides and allusions. One señora worked in a market stall growing up. Once every two years, politicians used to bus her to the *zócalo*—the Mexico City central plaza—then tell her to stand on a chalk mark, and cheer "¡viva!" whenever the party candidate paused.

Slipping with a boyfriend across the border one morning, she found work two thousand miles north, driving a tractor all night in beet fields. That first season, she saw other women leave their babies asleep at field's edge. At sunup, they had to locate the babies by the racket the kids made crying. Twenty years later, Cuca has acquired a green card and a mobile home. And international economics has multiplied her case by several hundred thousand. In the form of immigrants both devout and irreverent, gracious and self-contained, generous and unforgiving, La Reconquista is reaching the Inland Empire.

❊   ❊   ❊   ❊   ❊

The phrase "Inland Empire" appeared as early as 1848, when it graced the pages of George H. Atkinson, a congregational missionary hired to write a geologic report. The reverend no doubt figured that his words would lend an exotic cast to this land of sagebrush basin and ponderosa slope. From the Cascades to the Rockies, through eastern Washington and western Montana, northeastern Oregon and northern Idaho, a century and a half of habit and self-interest there bound the phrase—in the common mind—to tar-paper and tin-roof dreams, gravel-road and blue-sky optimism.

The phrase "La Reconquista," in contrast, was sterner stuff. Originating in Spain, it had first denoted the slow retaking of Christendom from infidel hands. In the New World, though, the phrase acquired a raw, insouciant tone. It managed to promise some righting of wrongs done to native people during La Conquista, the term that Spanish reserved for what English called, with airy detachment, the Discovery of the Americas. As street politics, La Reconquista even implied that Mexican nationals—in settling in the Inland Empire—were merely reclaiming land the United States had stolen from Mexico. A phrase sardonic and populist, derivative and opportunistic, La Reconquista designated a series of thrusts and parries, the cultural give and take, which enlivened the landscape at the moment. By tired guys in baseball caps with a six-pack in a parking lot, by women in braids hunting dented cans of food in the Safeway aisle, the phrase was used. But with a wink.

They referred to themselves simply as *mexicanos*. And certainly, when the term appeared in print, the italics and lowercase *m* helped remind the Anglo reader that no word in English quite captured what it was to be them: English had no word to refer to the simple fact of Mexican descent, no matter which side of the border you lived on. "Among ourselves," Gloria Anzaldúa writes, "we don't say *nosotros los americanos*, . . . *o nosotros los hispanos*. We say *nosotros los mexicanos* (by *mexicanos* we do not mean citizens of Mexico; we do not mean a national identity, but a racial one)." Although, as Anzaldúa admits, people do distinguish "between *mexicanos del otro lado* and *mexicanos de este lado*," mexicanos/as come from either side of the border.

The mexicanos in question inhabited what were traditional Western boomtowns. Except that the boom owed to high-quality, inexpensive mexicano labor, demand for which propelled whole families three thousand miles north to sleep in chicken coops and to dine in dirt-floor garages. On her first day here, any señora noticed orchards to prune, weedy trailer parks to live in, schools for kids. A year later, she might explain to her cousin—himself newly arrived—that even if your family came half a century before, nothing but mexicano energy and diligence accounted for your being here. Without documentation, day and night subject to being handcuffed and deported to the border—at least to where the U.S. government *thought* the border was—immigrants woke beside back roads, or at orchard edge. They worked numbing hours. On Mexican holidays, or at weddings and wakes, *quinceañeras* and christenings, they kicked back. They gathered over soda pop and beer, pig parts sizzling in a copper vat. Couples side by side on a sofa carried outside for the occasion, toddlers underfoot, teenagers gangly in folding chairs.

Nothing less than pioneer spirit sustained them. Theirs was a pure immigrant glee, the conviction that ambition and humility, the qualities that ought to count, did indeed count here where there was work, somewhere to live, and a chance to send back for loved ones. But everybody knew they'd come to a volatile place, one so unpredictable that even its name depended on which side of the border you viewed it from. If the gringos had always called it *The West*, to mexicanos it always had been *el norte*. So by the time La Reconquista hit the

Inland Empire, both phrases shared a descent, however indirect, from stuff like Manifest Destiny and Tierra y Libertad. No wonder both phrases rolled off your tongue.

✻   ✻   ✻   ✻   ✻

Mexico was born old. By the 1980s, it floated through history in ways the United States never would. Collective memory in Mexico—long and, of course, imperfect—got things wrong all the time, just as it did in the United States. But mexicano collective memory still saw Mexico as a child of La Conquista. It recalled Mexico's birth five hundred years before, during a century that saw the death of maybe as many as twenty-nine million out of thirty million native people. Examining archived copies of *Las Relaciones Geográficas*, the first census of the Americas, scholars still speak of an eighty percent plunge in native population in the Mexican highlands, the region that provided most of the Inland Empire's immigrants. *Las Relaciones* bristled with ambiguity. The same mix of deadpan and slapstick, the tone you heard batted back and forth through the migra van's protective screen—that very blend of entrapment and self-control prevailed, collective memory knew, in the voices that made up the first census data. It all started on a day in Madrid in 1580, a day when Felipe II, deep in his gray-granite, thousand-window palace, ordered that all of New Spain fill out a questionnaire. "In the pueblos of the Spaniards, let it be noted," the royal mustache twitched, "if there are many or few Indians, and whether in other times there have been more or fewer."

Half a world away, in what would become the state of Michoacán—later the source of millions who migrated north—the royal resolve wiggled in every which direction. Collective memory watched it permeate forest and lake, jungle and seashore until it reached tiny cornfields poked with a sharp stick into hillsides. Collective memory watched fresh-faced bureaucrats, guys not yet born when the Spaniards arrived, as they rode into village after village, to pluck mud off their leggings and clear their throats. The king's questions yielded the same vista again and again. When some young bureaucrat—call him José María—arrived, drum rolls and trumpet fanfare crowded his thinking. José María was starring in what felt to him like a scene out of *Amadís of Gaul*, that series of chivalric high jinks Spanish publishers trained on a readership still laced in doublets and scripture. José María's mind lay tucked away in imagination's saddlebags. Giants and enchantments. He was breathless. Call it passion's calisthenics.

On the other side of the interview, collective memory placed an eighty-year-old priest. Caltzonzín had no idea what these questions had to do with him. If the land seems healthy or ill and if ill, for what cause, if such be understood. How they govern themselves, and with whom they make war, and how they do battle. Caltzonzín would rather have told how the lake in front of him fell from the sky. Sure, the thing lay there lapping canoes nowadays. But once, it had shattered on contact with earth. Freshwater springs spurted. Nets leaped into people's hands. That's the kind of talk Caltzonzín would have used to characterize himself and where he was from. Collective memory was sure about that.

❊　❊　❊　❊　❊

The Purépecha Empire that the Spaniards found owed to recent migrations north from Andean lands. Savor the irony. The newest Purépecha wave had been in place a scant three centuries, archaeologists think nowadays, on that day when cannons roared, horses pranced, and the emperor—after one astonished look—surrendered to save bloodshed. He watched his empire become a colony. Suddenly, among reduced survival strategies, those of the merchant thrived. Commercial footpaths filled with men carrying—on their backs in baskets woven from reeds—salt and cocoa, fish and fruits and vegetables, grains and cotton and clothing. Maps still reflect what informants said in 1580 were the trade routes: a confusing whirl of curves and spirals, footpaths adapting to a market expanded, suddenly, by the Spanish Conquest.

Imagine how long a history there is to moving valuable merchandise over that resistant Mexican landscape. In the pre-Columbian world, *tamemes*, or merchants, hauled their goods on their back, supporting it all by a tumpline around the forehead. They were held in such respect that they enjoyed a kind of diplomatic immunity. The

Conquest intervened, and now those who put on the back frame and tumpline were mere slaves, unfortunates known by the bald patch the head-harness rubbed in, or the scalp ulcers it left. Enter pack animals, and the world changed again. The unimaginable wealth that poured into Felipe II's Spain owed to the labor of men half a world away, the *arrieros*, or pack train drivers. As mining interests in Mexico created the need for goods to be shipped overland, independent drover types began driving trains from Michoacán to the mining country to the north, then returning. By the 1740s they were journeying to states like Durango and Zacatecas, carrying rice, garbanzos, boots, etc. They brought back wool, hides, horses, and the like. Theirs was a world of intricate knots and foreign words. Their least little mistake dropped a mule thousands of feet off a mountain trail a few inches wide, bags of cinnamon roped to its back. Arrieros soon became Mexico's equivalent of New England's worldly, seafaring folk. The California gold fields in the late 1840s attracted thousands of arrieros, guys who returned wearing gringo clothing, having seen and talked to Frenchmen, Russians, Germans. Frequently they learned blacksmithing or masonry, a trade they plied when their wandering days were done.

The arriero wanders the national imagination, even today. Films and songs and novels have left him expressing mexicano adaptive powers. But the most demanding adaptation of all occurred very recently, sometime during the last half century, when Mexico's economy snapped, and the arrieros' own bodies became their most valuable merchandise. A 1980s *arriera*—still at the whims of supply and demand—might move thousands of miles north or south. On her first trip to the border, she likely rode buses over a Mexican landscape she'd never seen. She saw men who had never learned to read a map sprint across the border at night, or cramp into car trunks, then navigate by landmarks, billboard to bridge to barn. She blinked at electric garage doors, at toilets that flushed automatically. If such folk didn't get caught, and if they got a job, their lives resolved into parallel, ongoing scenes—one in slow motion in a neighborhood or rancho, the other a blur of orchards and packing sheds and labor camps. Names like Chicago and Atlanta bubbled up in their talk.

❧   ❧   ❧   ❧   ❧

Felipe II ruled for forty-two years. He ordered one census after another and squandered immense wealth. Certain that he'd been divinely appointed to drub Protestantism out of existence, Felipe toiled day and night. He had an enamel head painted to look like his own, then set it in the royal armor propped on his reviewing stand. Then he locked himself away in a tiny office to correct the grammar on documents that brought the Kingdom of God nearer every day. His costliest sacrifice was the 140 ships he sent—eight years after his questionnaire—to punish the English on behalf of Holy Mother Church. Hulks off the French coast, shipwrecked Spanish sailors lynched by Irish mobs, the Spanish Armada's loss launched Spain on her famous decline. By the end of the next century, Spain would lose her wealth to drab, opportunistic countries such as England. In the century after, she'd lose her colonies to independence.

But not yet. First time had to dangle suspended for one hundred years. Imagine the slow decay of the modern world's first superpower. The era is called El Siglo de Oro, the Golden Age. It blended florid expressive powers, in painting and writing, with a certain agile sympathy, an eye and ear for the likes of Sancho Panza. For another hundred years, the drawing rooms of Seville, Europe's busiest port, were prowled by syphilitic hookers. Beautiful and deadly in velvet and silk and satin and gold braid, muslin and swanskin and flannel, they tightroped their way up and down the Golden Age with tiny steps. They veiled their faces to show but a single eye. The Virgin herself appeared at Holy Week in gold and jewels.

❧   ❧   ❧   ❧   ❧

This week, in Washington State's Yakima Valley, the Virgin appeared on the back of traffic signs, as if to show what adaptations mexicanos would kneel before. Tuesday's Yakima newspaper headlined four hundred mexicanos gathered the night before under an Interstate 82 sign on which a city cop had reported seeing "a Madonna." The paper described the "concentric lines in pink, blue, and yellow hues" that "local Hispanic believers" think represent the Virgin of Guadalupe. One Hispanic believer drove one hundred miles with his sister—plus her three children and a grandson—to capture the apparition on videotape. He thought it would be like a hologram in the air, all detailed, but it was just the outline. Even so it was a rush. Especially when his sister confessed she felt like bursting into tears.

In a sidebar, Department of Transportation engineers explained that aluminum highway signs bore a chemical film that kept them from oxidizing. And that the film over time formed a halo effect, a light-purple tinge that migrated to stress points on the metal's surface. The regional maintenance engineer didn't think the sign looked a bit like the Virgin, by the way. You must have had to use your imagination. Though maybe, he admitted, he was unenlightened. The manager of the plant that supplied the aluminum sheets assured everyone that they weren't treated by monks or anything. It was done by a bunch of folks in Alabama.

The Highway Police already had overtime into patrolling what they called *the ethnic situation*, twenty to thirty surveillance hours crackling back and forth over their frequencies. And business at the Burger King down the road doubled. And Wal-Mart flat sold out its Virgin candles. "We'll have to remove the signs if this keeps up," mused the regional engineer. "But if you take a sign down, would these people say we removed it from sacred ground?"

Hispanic believers certainly knew the Virgin when they saw her. A farmworker from Michoacán recalled a bolt of lightning splitting a tree and burning on the soft inner wood an image exactly like that on the sign. His wife reported feeling shivers when she gazed at the aluminum. Friends felt lighthearted, or felt heaviness in the heart. The sixteen-year-old daughter said she studied the pages in her Bible that corresponded to the serial numbers on the signs. When a skeptical teenage guy objected that stainless steel pans, heated a few times, develop the same colors, his mother assured everyone that the signs were a message that we should pray about the youth of today and disobedience.

And just who were these Hispanic believers? For ten minutes one afternoon, they were a teenage couple and their baby, plus a big guy in Levi's and shades with mustache and belly drooping, plus three little girls in patent leather shoes, and their grandmother in baseball cap and rebozo. Everybody crossed themselves. They left flowers potted and cut and plastic. In all, Hispanic believers left fifty-some candles in glass containers painted with different versions of the Virgin. Only her colors and upright posture stayed the same from glass to glass, a likeness afterimaging into the air. It resembled the shape overhead on the freeway sign. Which of course was why people came.

❀   ❀   ❀   ❀   ❀

As the Spanish Hapsburg monarchy dwindled to its last decades, it acquired a world-class chronicler. In the city of Seville, the year after Felipe II died, Diego Velázquez was born. For forty years he would make a living arranging the glamorous squalor all around him into immortal poses. Velázquez left a series of portraits of his sovereign, the grandson of Felipe II. Indeed, painter and model spent their whole adult lives together. Felipe IV was blond with a long jaw and troubled eyes. The stresses that overcame the king's features, canvas by canvas, owed to problems long since identified: his lack of a male heir, his thirty illegitimate children, his having inherited an aristocracy already taxed threadbare. Especially his marriage to a woman whose notion of fun involved releasing snakes on the floor of a crowded theater—because she liked to watch that aristocracy sprinting in every which direction.

But mainly it was that business of Holy Mother Church, the military expense of eradicating Protestantism. It stretched Felipe's face slack. When even Madrid's shopkeepers at last refused their king credit, he became a mask of down-at-the-heels noblesse oblige. Velázquez trained on his king, over the years, a pity mixed with what people by the end of Felipe's days were calling *el desengaño*, a hard-bought freedom from illusion. That the king wasn't a stronger or wiser or brighter man than he was, was because neither the age he represented nor the people he ruled were very strong or wise or bright.

❀   ❀   ❀   ❀   ❀

Velázquez's best-known study of the royal family was called *Las Meninas*, after the maids of honor who shared its foreground with a princess, two dwarves, and a dog. Velázquez portrayed himself in front of his sovereigns, painting. They themselves appeared—tiny, blurred—in a mirror over his left shoulder. As he worked, the princess's retinue collected underfoot, and filled the center of the canvas. Maybe he put her there because she alone, by posing in front of her parents, held their attention long enough for him to paint them.

Anyhow, it was my neighbor Cuca's favorite painting. She kept a tiny, blurred reproduction of it in a drawer, beside spare car keys and a rosary. The painting appeared on the back of a yellow matchbox, with the word *Clásicos* printed on the front. Tucked away deep in the drawer, trailing dog and dwarves and maids, the little blonde princess looked like she was about to melt into light. And at her side, the painter paused with brush midair, gaze distant, as if to consider the royal couple's take on the princess posed before them. We can't see the canvas he shows himself at work on. Maybe he was finishing the very piece in which they all now appeared, this canvas that let all those in it see themselves as pose, brushstroke, subject matter. Anybody could see el desengaño showing through their features.

My neighbor Cuca probably never noticed the Cross of Santiago gleaming on Velázquez's shirtfront. It indicated his elevation to the nobility, a triumph that in fact befell him long after he finished the painting. Legend says that Felipe IV himself—after Velázquez was dead—seized a brush and added those red slashes, awarding him posthumously an insignia that the painter had coveted for forty years. The Cross meant that Diego Velázquez had blood neither Moorish nor Jewish, and had lived as a gentleman always, and had never painted for a living. It was exactly the sort of wish that only a king could grant. For Cuca and Velázquez both, the word *real* meant both "royal" and "real."

❀   ❀   ❀   ❀   ❀

Legend by legend, La Conquista grew. At last it attracted reformers like don Vasco de Quiroga. Driven by a zeal he caught from reading Thomas More's *Utopia*, don Vasco finagled himself a job administering New Spain's *audiencia*, a post that had him listening to Indians' complaints about abuses of power. To this day, legend snaps at his deeds like a cheap camera: that he understood the gravity of his calling when—auditing his first complaint—he noticed the interpreters were weeping at the tale they stood there interpreting. In a letter we still have, a contemporary wrote the king that what don Vasco felt for Indians was "a visceral love." Certainly, it was a passion that wrenched thick stone blocks into place for schools and for hospices to die in. Legend again: him finding the site he wanted to found a town on—it was dry—and whacking a boulder with his bishop's rod until water gushed out.

Barefoot, in robes so heavily mended that contemporaries described men wearing more patch than fabric, don Vasco and those who followed him wandered. They left behind them naves and reliefs and *cupulas*, sacristies and baptismal fonts. Hiking alone from one native population to another, they learned exotic tongues in order to inculcate the word of God. Plus elementary hygiene and crop planting. As late as the 1980s, the small-town highland region that Cuca came from was full of cathedrals, temples, convents—stone that reminded the visitor that men like don Vasco had built to counteract the pyramids then looming on hilltop and shore. Penniless themselves, men like don Vasco wrangled what they needed from a frequently reluctant Church. Because they meant to dummy-up a glimpse of that eternal life that awaited the Christian soul? Maybe. They certainly built out of gold and silk, marble and ivory. Year after year, they flung up the walls and Roman arches that tinged Cuca's highlands pink to cream, purple to yellow—a massive, pastel indifference to weather and time. La Conquista grew until it vanished into people's thinking. It stranded the modern world between geographic relations and visceral love.

     ❊   ❊   ❊   ❊   ❊

The pueblos of La Reconquista—let it be noted—are now home to a race of arrieros. By the end of the 1980s, in collective memory, Inland Empire mexicanos descended from the scrappy folk who had transported the king's wealth, people who put that haunted look on the face of Felipe. The way that Velázquez painted his old friend of course was a trick, one depth illusion layered into another. And yet, receding waves of brushstroke and pose caught the passions of La Reconquista better than any photo, or any relief-globe perspective.

Don Vasco, of course, had brought the Lord to Indians by means of Roman arch and red roof tile. But this was a mobile age. La Virgen had wiggled into people's lives on the back of a traffic sign. In fact, one morning at the Yakima River Flea Market, the sun shone as bright as it ever had in Michoacán, on what people even here called *el tianguis*. Walking away from each other, mexicanos bargained in wide gestures, wisecracking, suffering in silence. Inside was a bin full of rubber sandals made in Korea, and boom boxes, and stacks of polyester pants, a card table of used cameras, a bathtub of used telephones, you name it. Wall heaters by women's underwear, plastic flowers by pincushions, followed by a stall full of dolls that closed their eyes and wet and cried, another of paper flowers and microwave pork-rind packages. Products to dummy up a glimpse of how good life could be? An automobile trunk full of nail polish and lipstick, neckties painted with outlines of states like Guerrero and Guanajuato.

At the end of a century when Congress had made deserts bloom, La Reconquista persisted. It kept emitting glimpses of itself like a homing signal.

2 Wets

A 1993 flood sent one of the rivers that form the U.S.-Mexican border wandering hundreds of yards out of its channel. Three years later, surveyors stand on opposite sides of the sticky expanse the flood left speculating where—amid all that mud—the international line really is. Their confusion is understandable. Even apart from the problem of flooding, water no longer reliably defines the boundary between the two countries. Decades of irrigation have disrupted the "normal flow" that treaties refer to. Reservoirs and canals and ditches on both sides of the border long ago distorted the border.

So the term "wet" is a throwback. It comes from an era when Mexicans slipped into this country to work by wading a body of water that Mexico calls the Rio Bravo. Anglos, of course, call it the Rio Grande—a modification which meant that, right from the start, irony trailed the wet. You got here by crossing a landmark that changed its name while you crossed it.

Even now, you never leave that half-assed irony behind. When you cross into the United States, Mexico clings like the odor of wood smoke to how you talk and dress. The tales that surround your getting here have you creeping into the country via culverts foul with sewage and rats. Or limping across whole days of desert, plucking cholla spines from your pant legs. The truth of the matter is often less vivid: many Mexicans come with money. In the pre–September 11 era of 1996, paying $750 to ride direct from border barbwire to apple orchard, they could pick up a pair of pruning shears and start earning a paycheck.

Here in the Cascade foothills, upwards of fifty thousand people inhabit the calculated blind spot the U.S. government trains on Mexico, on things Mexican. Though getting here is a problem. A typical pre–September 11 formula had the prospective immigrant traveling north to Tijuana, where a *coyote* would take a group of ten such folk across on a three-hour walk to a house in San Isidro. Since September 11, border surveillance has intensified enough that crossing routes are longer, harsher, often deadly. But whatever kind of crossing you endure, three days and nights on a floor follow, lying shoulder to shoulder among thirty other hopefuls, tiptoeing out only to pee, eating one meal a day and that only beans and eggs.

At last another *coyote* drives everyone—in groups of five—to the second and final checkpoint. Four ride jammed into the trunk, one crouches behind the front seat, and they drive right up to the checkpoint. The driver stops, and when the officer on duty approaches, grinds the accelerator, zipping past. Sometimes the migra will get so frustrated he or she will smack the rear windshield with that long-handled mirror they use to peek under cars. A couple of miles down the road, when the *coyote* shouts that they've made it, a round of applause ripples from inside the trunk.

❖   ❖   ❖   ❖   ❖

The presence of illegal aliens here in the Cascade foothills is due to factors economic and historical, to forces that come into play with all the rigor of those that thrust the canyons and ridges overhead. Economist Jorge Bustamente has characterized the issue of Mexican immigration as a matter of international economics, a question of the supply and demand of labor. And yet, he argues, it's an issue that keeps on being treated as if it were a U.S. political problem. The Simpson-Mazzoli Bill of 1982, for example, set out to pacify both growers and the ten percent of the U.S. labor force unemployed at the time: it promised to increase the number of INS agents, even while it liberalized the obtaining of work visas. The result was that growers exercised even more control over the foreign workers they employed. Meanwhile, the public believed the government had "done something" about illegal immigration—which indeed it had. The government had done nothing about the supply of cheap labor in Mexico, however, let alone about U.S. growers' demand for it.

Local wets tend to come from that part of the Mexican Central Highlands where Michoacán, Guanajuato, and Jalisco share a border. Their working this far north is a stage in a process that dates from at least 1909. In that year Jesús Fernández Hurtado, along with six other fellows, left Gómez Farías, Michoacán. Times were hard on the Guarucha hacienda where they worked. And they wanted to see the world. So, they took a train to Texas, found a labor contractor, and promptly became part of the Michoacán labor force that helped lay five thousand miles of U.S. railroad tracks in 1910.

They came back changed men. They wore bib overalls and boots now, rather than the huaraches and loose, white-cotton trousers they left in. Neighbors came by the dozen to hear their tales of el norte. By 1925, Gustavo López Castro writes, the sons of those first adventurers were heading north to work in the fields. For their journey, they needed only proof that they were solid citizens in search of honest work. Arriving at the border, they were given a bath, and then charged eighteen dollars for a passport that let them work in the United States.

The flow of immigration north from Gómez Farías diminished during the early thirties, when the Guarucha hacienda was being parceled into small farms. By the early forties, though, a scarcity both of land and money—as well as the labor demand created by World War II—sent men from Gómez Farías back to the United States to work in fields outside Watsonville, California, serving as part of the Bracero Program. Ensuing decades have seen ever more U.S. acreage brought under cultivation, with both the production and the *michoacanos* who make it possible reaching ever farther north. Sometimes local wets amount to the fourth or fifth consecutive generation that a family has sent to work U.S. crops. Orchards, as well as fields of asparagus and hops, account for central Washington State being home to the fastest-growing mexicano population in the country.

Gómez Farías today, meanwhile, owes much of how it looks to

the fact that eighty-seven percent of its families have seen the father leave at least once to work in the United States. The dollars they earn result in older, adobe houses being replaced by newer homes of brick and concrete, the walls of which even bear murals their owners have commissioned from an enterprising local artist. Some nine hundred letters a month arrive in Gómez Farías from the United States, bearing both money and news from loved ones. A local radio station even airs a program entitled *La hora del ausente*, which reads messages from—and plays tunes requested by—those at work up north. From gang graffiti to fertilizers to calendars featuring views of the Rocky Mountains, U.S. influence leaks into Gómez Farías. Dollars earned in the United States are at work remodeling the plaza. López Castro reports that sixty-six percent of the kids in the grade school want to work in the United States.

❖   ❖   ❖   ❖   ❖

Deeper than any outward transformation of towns like Gómez Farías, changes accumulate in the minds of those who leave to go north. Wets acquire certain sensitivities. They bristle with vigilance. Today as I eat lunch in a local bar—under the stuffed heads of an eight-point buck, an elk, a moose—four illegal aliens from Mexico are serving food. Renting the kitchen, they've opened a small restaurant—their own business, independent of the bar. Now a couple of cops saunter in. They mean no harm, they're making their rounds. But the guys behind the stove—not so much as a fake ID among them—stiffen and eye the back door. To dodge trouble with bosses and landlords, spiteful co-workers and self-righteous neighbors, wets maintain a supernormal range of hearing.

The minute the cops are out the door, the guys are working again, elbow to elbow, grinding cheese and boiling chilis, dicing pork and browning tortillas, gossiping, snickering, reminiscing. Their hands flicker from lettuce to onion, olive to cilantro. They chat about the Labor Day Rodeo Weekend crowd out the window—Seattle orthodontists in chaps, tax lawyers in lizard-skin boots. When a mexicano goes by on the sidewalk, bearing a girl on his arm, the topic turns.

to countrymen who leave wives behind when they come up here to work.

Someone recalls working with a youngster who married a girl, and then left her ten days later to pick apples up north. When the crew found out he was newly married and sending money back home, the jeers flew from ladder to ladder: "Ah buey, a poco vas a mandar dinero pa' atrás? Así nomás mantienes a el que te está poniendo los cuernos." The kid didn't last a week—victim to the stress that wears a country boy down. The constant threat of deportation subjects you to a floating, impermanent feel. Even while you yawn or swallow, comb your hair or tie a shoelace, your surroundings assume the unreal air of stuff that can vanish at a blink.

Of course living wet offers consolations as well. However much you feel trapped in a system austere and impersonal, U.S. authority—disquieting thing that it is—feels strangely reassuring too. It doesn't demand bribes, after all. One of the guys in the kitchen recalls to the others how construction workers in Mexico City came on Saturdays to a certain building to be paid. Knowing they had money, the traffic police circled outside like flies, poised to write them tickets. The fellow swears he'd run home with his salary tucked in his shoe, and then kneel inside the front door at his mother's shrine to the Virgin, whispering thanks.

My friends appreciate the lack of corruption here. In general, they feel that their toil is rewarded more reliably here than it ever was in the old country. They speak of the relative lack of exploitation as "opportunity," as "chances to get ahead."

❊   ❊   ❊   ❊   ❊

The border demands certain personality traits of the people who cross it. But the unfamiliarity of the crossing makes it hard for wets to recount. It blurs into freeway ramps and interchanges, convenience stores and fast-food joints. Nobody navigates with a map. Traveling across this country, illegal aliens generally don't know what lies between where they are and the village they come from. Crossing is above all a matter of having sufficient nerve. Think of those Spanish soldiers of fortune who sixteenth-century chronicles portray, lounging in a pyramid's shade, shuffling cards they cut from the skins on their drums.

And yet it's a rare book that conveys the whiplash quality of undocumented life. Two wholly different views have to be joined: a U.S. perspective needs to coexist with that of the immigrant. Consider two books: Ted Conover's *Coyotes*, and Ramón "Tianguis" Pérez's *Diary of an Undocumented Immigrant*. Conover is an Amherst College graduate, author of a book on hobos and another on prison guards. Pérez, on the other hand, reared in a village in Oaxaca, comes off as a shrewd country boy prowling the 1980s United States.

Conover always knows where he is. He managed to meet young crop pickers and field hands from a small town in Michoacán. He followed them to agricultural jobs in Arizona, Florida, and Wyoming. Covering two thousand miles of icy roads in a car with bald tires, he's conscious every moment that they haven't any map, that they're driving a route committed to memory. Pérez, though he covers nearly as many miles, scarcely seems to notice. He plods back and forth, Houston to L.A., Oregon to Orange County. For Pérez the journey is isolated stopovers, meals and rooms shared with people who wash dishes or cars, who change sheets or mop floors—free-floating, lucid scenes hinged by a babble he can't understand.

Conover's month visiting his friends at home in Michoacán reveals one effect of so much migration. We see a social structure in ruins, at least according to the parish priest who describes a community breakdown due to adult males leaving to work in the United States. Wives and children are abandoned. Teenage girls run off with married men and come back pregnant. The United States seems to have, on that village in Michoacán, an effect like what the frontier had on nineteenth-century towns that furnished the labor force for Manifest Destiny.

Pérez, in contrast, celebrates the indestructibility of mexicano communities newly born in the United States. In the L.A. area several hundred *oaxaqueños* from his hometown attend each other's weddings and christenings. They phone each other for loans and advice.

Within hours, the news of any event of importance that transpires back home reaches L.A. The oaxaqueños living in L.A. form a kind of village outskirts, municipal limits transposed onto a richer, more fluid backdrop.

Conover's book dates from 1987, and that of Pérez from four years later. But my neighbors experience the very same features of distance and incongruity, coherence and connection, alienation and networking.

❊   ❊   ❊   ❊   ❊

Fracaso is a tricky word in Spanish. English-speaking folk often suppose it has to do with "fracas," a word to which it is no doubt related. But *un fracaso* is something like a splashy, public failure, not as serious as a disaster, but far more grave than simply having *problemas*.

This week the restaurant business was a fracaso. Central Plateau individualism surfaced again. The guys running the restaurant work hard, but something in them resists the organizing of individual effort either in time or in space.

The restaurant is in the hands of four partners, two of them straight from a small town in the back-country state of Nayarit, each in his mid-twenties. The other two, in their mid-forties, have been all over Mexico as well as a lot of the U.S. West. After a feeling-out period, the four began to work in the pairs I describe—the young in one shift, the middle-aged in the other—and promptly started arguing recipes and ingredients. Finally some cash wound up missing from the till. Blame was directed and huffily denied. The air turned rigid.

I know all four pretty well. They're amiable, considerate, and plain good company. So I wince when they can't get along with each other. Or I mean the gringo version of me winces. The mexicano version turns palms up, wondering what I expected out of such contentious, eccentric folk. Notice that the two versions judge from angles truly irreconcilable, even though strangely complementary. I can't maintain both perspectives at once.

The irreducible individualism I'm talking about amounts to resistance to regulations. One night, one partner comes in half an hour late, beaming that he's here a bit tardy but reliable as always. Another decides one night, on closing, simply not to open for breakfast the next morning, since eggs really shouldn't be fried on that griddle but rather in a Teflon-coated skillet—which of course he doesn't have, so *ni que* breakfast.

Around a great deal of what my friends do, the Anglo perspective detects a halo of irony—but wait. The "Anglo perspective" I call it only for convenience's sake. After all, mexicanos turn an ironic gaze on themselves all the time. So what would happen if I read these very paragraphs to my four friends? Their first reaction would be to sizzle in angry recrimination over who did what to whom.

And if I pointed out that their reaction exemplifies the same perverse individualism that my paragraphs attribute to them? Why, they'd grin and shrug. A flair for self-scrutiny runs very deep in my friends. A certain mexicano passion for seeing the self as alternately tragic and farcical prevails, and makes for a dizzying group identity. The youngsters of wet parents are reared to think of themselves as descended from a fickle race—individuals characterized by courage and reserve, people who also seek each other out to form groups and bicker.

The same individualism makes it hard to keep on schedule. The very concept skids off my friends' thinking. The guys ask me to help them out, so we sit for an hour putting names in time slots. But it is a constant test of wills. My friends keep bringing up larger issues, the nature of free enterprise, for example, opining that any individual willing to work can succeed in this country. Me, I keep wrenching our focus back to hours and days. Until at last the guys say, "yeah, that's ok." They hitch up their pants and amble off, never even glancing at the schedule I drew up.

Which leaves me feeling about like you'd expect. Because I'm the one left to explain to the Anglo bar owner how come my flaky friends are late or missing. Until at last there's nothing for it but to pick a quiet hour, pull a stool into the kitchen and crack open a Diet Coke, and get in on the talk Rubén and Beto are having about the free enterprise system.

❊   ❊   ❊   ❊   ❊

My friends are risk addicts, irony mongers. Something in them senses that the world is a place inhospitable to the aspirations one enters it with. So running off to el norte—to where both opportunity and hardship abound—remains after four centuries an act that represents the mixed feelings *la raza* has about the world, in ever finer distinctions of attitude and accent. Consider it the friction of subplots, or a preference for mixed feelings: it explains why the United States—a land of abundance and sacrifice, of fortune and fracaso—presents a tangy blend of attributes more attractive to mexicanos than milk and honey. In 1996, up and down the Cascade foothills, in the fastest-growing Hispanic population in all the United States, getting deported cost only a couple of weeks, and a couple hundred dollars. So what if they had no idea what they were getting into? Wets were thriving, weren't they?

Well, yes and no. After six weeks of toil, for example, the guys finally closed the kitchen, having lost money the whole time. They said the college kids they hoped to attract did begin showing up, but they'd order only a couple of tacos, then sit belching and feeling exotic. Remember, above all, that the United States sends most wets home disappointed. On wrought-iron park benches in Mexico's central highlands, elderly men and women nod over memories of some Arizona mining town, some Kansas City slaughterhouse, the Jeep factory in Toledo, the sugar beet fields outside Boise. Little pieces of history chipped off by the wrenching effects of peso devaluation or land redistribution, their memories amount to the active ingredient in immigration to the United States. Their memories keep U.S. economic promise as fresh in the air as the odors of jasmine and diesel exhaust.

My friends, though, are still here. They've resumed the jobs they had pruning apple trees or sweeping floors, nailing apple crates or washing dishes. All that is except for Oscar, who swilled half a liter of tequila week before last, then took off in a borrowed car, only to be arrested. Now he's awaiting the deportation that is sure to provide him with one more border-crossing story.

Changeable as the border itself, mexicano migration proceeds. It reminds you of country folk teetering across a creek, each fracaso a balance recovered, a recapitulation a bit askew. No wonder that that original trip north, the one that gave wets their name, took *mi raza* over water. The Rubicon and the River Styx had nothing on what some people cross to get here. Afterward, what lies between you and what you were? Water that changed its name the moment you crossed it.

3   Postcards from Michoacán

Erica mops floors and washes windows in the house I'm staying in. She's twenty-two, a kid with Hollywood-regular features, fair skin, and black hair that she ties in a ponytail. She sniffs a forever-drippy nose. Her voice takes on a high, singsong note as she wipes the leaves of plants on the patio.

She confides that a neighbor boy got her in bed with a single promise: they'd run off to The Other Side—they'd live and work in the United States. She saw herself in designer jeans and sunglasses, floating from one magazine pose to another. But the guy married a friend of hers instead, and then left for the apple orchards in Washington State. Now she lives with her parents and three sisters in a two-bedroom apartment. While she scrubs toilets, her parents wholesale cheese to markets and stores.

Out the front window, across the street, brass fittings gleam on the wrought-iron gate of don Kiko. At age fifty he lives from November to February here in a house built with proceeds from the catering business that he and his wife have run for twenty years outside Yakima. At the height of the picking season up there—he told me once—they sleep maybe an hour a night, stewing pork and patting tortillas, loading a couple hundred breakfasts into the pickup camper they drive to the orchards at dawn, then returning to sack the lunches they have to have in the fields by one o'clock.

So these are the days that don Kiko kicks back. He sleeps late, and then phones old friends. A slender fellow in pressed khakis and polo shirt, tiny mustache and aviator glasses, he waxes his pickup in the street, then sips a couple of evening beers in front of his thirty-inch TV. Twenty years ago, he was climbing apple ladders, pruning and thinning and picking. Now he eats off a three-thousand-dollar dining room set.

*　　*　　*　　*　　*

The lives of Erica and Kiko intersect in the city of Morelia, in Michoacán State—the source, whether directly or at a few generations' remove, of some twenty million people currently living in the United States. Founded in 1540, Morelia features green parks and colonial architecture that have drawn four and a half centuries of admiring remarks. They've also drawn fifty years of steady immigration from the surrounding countryside.

Kiko and Erica—like most of the folk who move to Morelia—were born in two of the countless small towns scattered through the surrounding hills. Over the last half-century, such folk have kept the city growing exponentially; its yearly growth rate—3.6 percent from 1940 to 1950—rising in the next twenty years to 4.8 percent, and then during the following twenty to 6.8 percent.

The current population of more than half a million strains the schools and the water supply, the systems of garbage and sewage disposal. Country folk who come to the city wind up living in squatter camps, shantytowns without electricity or drinking water, with sewage trickling down the dirt streets.

Paracaidistas, people call them. Their cardboard walls and flattened–tin-can roofs sprout on your fallow cornfield, or on your empty corner lot. And you have to call the police, who come and tear down everything, except that the paracaidistas come back, and before long have cinder-block walls and galvanized metal roofs. And by now there's five thousand of them. So the police won't go in. You have to call the army, which costs money you don't want to spend. So a new neighborhood is founded.

*　　*　　*　　*　　*

The growth of Morelia hurts your eyes. It's a road-flare of baroque incongruity. Irony refracts what you can see of this exquisitely kept-up city. Consider the ordinance mandating colonial architecture for all downtown buildings: streets teem with the recently arrived, who neither know nor care that from 1810 to 1820 this state cradled the War of Independence.

Erica, for example, can't even read the bronze plaque marking the birthplace museum of Morelos—a mestizo priest who led mestizo troops in a brilliant campaign against the Spaniards—much less appreciate the conflicting memorabilia that the fellow left behind. One day a Spanish firing squad made him immortal. Behind glass, today, we see the hemp scourge he flailed himself with. Portraits of his three illegitimate children. A gold-plated shepherd staff propped on leather-bound volumes of Voltaire.

The visitor who knows what to look for can sense, in the good father, a familiar clash: doubt sideswiping faith. Morelos recalls the sad, ambivalent whiskey priest in Graham Greene's *The Power and the Glory*. But when I mention Morelos to Kiko, he isn't sure who the guy was. He thinks that maybe Father Morelos fought in World War II.

Morelia's incongruities grow on you. Convents turned into libraries, sacristies into post office branches, the anticlerical overtones that have always caught the visitor's eye recede ever farther from those of us who live here now, native and immigrant alike. The downtown—thick blocks of pink cantera stone in rows—begins to feel both permanent and momentary.

Morelia teeters on the edge of things. It is and always has been a province of the Valley of Mexico. The local airport isn't as busy as the one in Mexico City. Morelia's cathedral isn't nearly as grand as its counterpart in Mexico City. Despite its growth, Morelia still has fewer people. After all, by now one of every three Mexicans lives in or around the Valley of Mexico.

Morelia's growth leaves the city a province in another sense as well. It depends on the United States every bit as much as it does on the Valley of Mexico. Two and a half million dollars in Social Security benefits arrive every year for Michoacán folk retired from U.S. jobs.

*   *   *   *   *

Parked at the curb out front one night, behind the wheel of his camper, a coffee cup of pulque in his hand, Fernando doesn't want to talk. He's maybe 25 years old, a thin, fuzzy beard blurring his round cheeks. He wears Levi's, a San Francisco 49'ers T-shirt, a baseball cap. One front tooth wears a silver cap with a star shape cut in it. A neighbor told me that he's the guy who got Erica in bed.

Edgy, eying first me and then the keys in the ignition, he answers in monosyllables. No, he's never been a bracero. No, it isn't his truck. In fact, he doesn't even know whether the pulque in his cup is any good, since he's never drunk pulque before.

And yet when I mention I'm writing a book, he figures out I'm not a cop. And he's grinning with glee. Hell yes, he's gone to The Other Side—oranges in Florida, tomatoes in Illinois. As soon as the foreman phones to say the branches are free of ice, he and his cousins will head to Wenatchee to prune.

A dollar in the hand is worth one hundred pesos in the bush, Fernando grins. In the old days, our wives wept when we left to work up north. Now they weep if we don't.

*   *   *   *   *

Kiko and Erika were born in a hamlet high in the sierra, an area that comprises maybe two-thirds of the state of Michoacán. It is a place where people dwell outside the national network of roads and highways, beyond the reach of sewer or electric lines. Unschooled, unchurched, drinking unpurified water, they coax a living from plots of farmland that slope as much as forty or fifty degrees. Erosion gnaws at the soil. Weeds invade. There's no shade.

To feed chickens, pigs, and cattle, each family plants a plot, or *parcela*, in spring at the end of the dry season. After clearing the brush with machetes, burning it down to a soil so stony that plows are worthless, the campesino stabs kernels of corn in the ground—using the same kind of fire-hardened stick that people here, five centuries ago, placed each year on an altar, and sprinkled drops of pulque on, and offered ceremonial thanks to. After each harvest, sometimes for as long as ten years, the steep, rocky plot lies fallow.

No wonder michoacanos emigrate! Consider a parcela acquired during the Reparto Agrario, the land redistribution of the 1930s. It began as a plot intended to help one family become self-sufficient landowners, but half a century later, inherited and divided several times, its hold on those who worked it was tenuous. Every single one of that original owner's heirs, by the 1980s, also depended on seasonal work in mills, factories, refineries. Then the government devalued the peso and quit subsidizing small farms. From that point on, whole families started heading north.

But before that point, when mainly young men went, going to el norte was a way of life. Sharecroppers, shopkeepers, anybody up for a long shot, *pero nada de gente delicada*—el norte wasn't for the fainthearted. At the beginning of the century, for example, it attracted thousands of *arrieros,* those intrepid Mexican teamsters now thrown out of work by the very railroad that made going north so easy. For half a century, el norte was an itch, a deep urge everyone respected. Isaac Gallegos, now eighty-two, recalls setting out on foot at age fifteen one night, yelling with his buddies, "Chin' a su madre el que no se vaya pa'l norte." Anyone not heading north was an asshole.

　　　＊　　＊　　＊　　＊　　＊

Kiko and Erika come from a rancho of three thousand people, one that sends young men north in greater numbers every year to plant and prune, pick and pack, to get bored and drunk and lonely, and wish they were back home.

Erika and Kiko draw my attention because, between them, they represent convenient extremes, the migrant poised to flee the country, the migrant returned prosperous. Viewed close-up, however, their lives reveal the usual difficulties small-town people have adapting to city life.

Everybody knows that Erika has occasional sex with the corner butcher—at one hundred pesos a plunge—and barely finished the sixth grade in special education. She can't count the bills she is handed, and doesn't know where she and her parents live, except to say it's in a yellow apartment on Bus Line #4. Kiko, for his part, behind his manicured image of self-made worth, leads a life his family talks around, never about. Kiko has a *casa chica*. In an apartment downtown live the four children Kiko's had with a woman that, he shrugs, is cute in the dark.

❊   ❊   ❊   ❊   ❊

People fleeing hillside life make Morelia what it is: the largest city in a state where the primary export is the migrant labor it supplies both to Mexican cities and to the United States. Attention split between U.S. and Mexican perspectives, no wonder the city blurs its past and its present.

Walk through a construction project still teeming with workers newly arrived from small towns. In their straw hats and dusty boots, their country twang and deferential demeanor, they release a feel of bygone stability. Stand under the Roman arches of the eighteenth-century aqueduct. Listen as the repairmen lean on their shovels and chat. You feel caught in the late nineteenth century. And yet for nearly one hundred years, that very kind of guy has gone north and returned with new words and clothing styles and eating habits. These country boys have brought the future to Michoacán.

All over the state, in the small towns they come from, migrants back nowadays from the United States build houses of brick, bungalows that stand out among the adobe huts all around them, their galvanized or shingle roofs contrasting with those of tile. The migrants' houses have yards, not patios. From three thousand miles north, a steady rain of money orders fascinates the neighbors—indoor plumbing and picture windows and gas stoves. English words sprout in the talk of schoolchildren.

A kind of psychological migration even takes over downtown Morelia. Dealers in contraband crowd the central plaza with plywood tables. In the form of logos that come from far away, they sell a thin sense of isolation: the Looney Tunes beach balls and Nike socks, Chicago Bulls bookbags and Elizabeth Taylor perfume. It all radiates a hip, utterly self-absorbed air—if only when displayed next to the copper and clay flowerpots that locals turn out, the coconut candy, the bamboo letter openers. And yet, it's nothing new. The elderly still recall how early migrant workers left wearing white cotton pants and shirts and huaraches, only to return in boots, bib overalls, and denim jackets. Some even came back brandishing pocket watches.

❖   ❖   ❖   ❖   ❖

Migration, not surprisingly, won't resolve into a permanent picture. Michoacán is nobody's case history yet. Take those logos downtown on the plywood tables. They are used without permission. A tradition of gleefully pirating U.S. images keeps thousands of Mexicans busy in shops every bit as established, and nearly as native to these parts, as those of coppersmith and candymaker. The potter firing and painting Christmas tree ornaments, and the Indian shaving wooden souvenirs with a broken bottle, counterpoint a teenager silk-screening T-shirts with phrases he can't pronounce.

Rumors abound that corporations like Nike and Disney plan to enforce NAFTA provisions protecting copyrights. But nobody seems too worried. How long, after all, could those fellows afford to hang around? Pirated U.S. images leak into daily life here with the same steady stealth that illegal aliens nip across the U.S. border.

Is it that kind of constant exposure that erodes the border, then, and sets Mexicans to migrating—toward destinations both national and international? Who knows. Most of what you read is guesswork.

The arguments I cite above–for example, the painful ups and downs of hillside farming–are derived from scanty data. Most census takers, everybody admits, simply don't bother to trudge for three or four days in order to count the children and chickens, measure the eroded topsoil, and note which family members have left to pour concrete to build Morelia convention centers or to pick asparagus outside some unpronounceable gringo town. The census taker makes an educated guess, and turns in data which then form a basis for the more sophisticated guesswork we call social science.

❖   ❖   ❖   ❖   ❖

An Irish friend, a woman who knows both countries, tried to explain her homeland to me once in a single phrase. Ireland, she said, was the Mexico of Europe: the absent workers and the poverty left a haunting note in the voice, a feeling strung between admiration and hate. Did she mean that gringos are to Mexico what the British are to Ireland? Sure, she raised her glass. Why not?

Because, of course, Mexico isn't a single pair of antagonisms. The state of Michoacán yields everything but beginnings and ends. Here when fields are plowed, or sewer lines dug, it is earlier loyalties that turn up. Purépechas and Spaniards and the French, the Mexican Reform and dictatorship and Mexican Revolution, *mexicano* history comes down to a shifty series of histories. Authority flares and fizzles.

❖   ❖   ❖   ❖   ❖

Framed photos of the last fifty municipal presidents hang on a limestone wall in city hall, in Erika and Kiko's hometown. They're fellows whose fashion sense ranges from celluloid collars to guayaberas, from denim jackets to the incumbent's three-piece suit. At the door a municipal cop stands, sporting a black baseball cap and a disdainful look. Plus a black T-shirt, black trousers tucked in black combat boots with white laces, and a snub-nose .38 tucked into an empty cartridge belt.

This morning, two authorities arrive from Morelia to pick up paperwork from a government project. The government is paying to remodel a hacienda into city hall, La Presidencia Municipal, so two officials have come for receipts and cancelled checks. It's a documentation that everyone knows is slanted, shaded. But there are limits after all.

Enter authority #1, the Ingeniero. He grins and shakes hands and elbows a few ribs. He's wearing designer jeans, shirt unbuttoned halfway to the navel, a customized key chain dangling from his front pocket. The Licenciado follows. He's thin, reserved, with a thick mustache, clicking his ballpoint pen. He carries a spiral binder with a Snoopy cover.

It turns out that the president is at home in bed, still droopy from yesterday's celebration of the beginning of Lent: a parade replete with two marching bands, four papier-mâché bulls, and truly prodigious amounts of pulque. So the visitors send a boy to fetch the president.

They wait. People in straw hats and aprons wander the patio shaking hands, receiving the five-kilo bags of cornmeal the government gives away, and then paying their water bill or light bill.

Forty-five minutes later, the president eases in the back door.

The voice of the president takes on a hurt note at the merest hint that maybe a few receipts are missing. Licenciado and Ingeniero step outside to smoke and study their shoelaces. What sort of fine to assess the municipal president? He is after all but a second-grade graduate. But paperwork was due last month.

Meanwhile, the president sprawls on a bench, picks his teeth with a thorn, and sighs that the funds were well spent, no matter what some effete accountant might think.

✳   ✳   ✳   ✳   ✳

Across the plaza stands the church, built by fifteenth-century Augustine missionaries—and on its patio walls, a curious mural. The missionaries apparently told skilled Indian artisans that they wanted portrayed, on these patio walls, the sort of depredations that the order had suffered in the New World. And depredations were what they got. To this day the black-robed friars on those walls are getting their heads lopped off. A few, piteously bleeding, aim mournful glances at the sky.

Something's not quite right though. Because a closer glance reveals that those inflicting the damage look rather like Spaniards. They're fair-skinned fellows with beards. They wear doublets and hose and breastplates. They brandish swords.

I think about those fifteenth-century Michoacán artisans a lot. How come they represented friars dying at the hands of Spaniards? An architect friend tells me they were recording a specific slaughter of friars by Spanish troops, news of which was quickly suppressed. The sexton figures, *pos' no*, maybe they just didn't know how to draw Indians.

Maybe somewhere a single, definitive reading of those walls exists, a state-of-the-art version of what the fifteenth century had in mind. But my guess is, nobody knows.

4 Don Diego's Book

Consider the cruel mirth that made up the life of don Diego Durán, a priest who lived four and a half centuries ago. In Texcoco, right across the lake from what would become Mexico City, don Diego was born into an era of pitiless syncretism, the grinding into particles and recombining which Roman Catholic belief went through at the Spanish Conquest. A generation after the Spaniards' invasion, he grew up fluent in both Spanish and Náhuatl. He died in 1588, the year the Spanish Armada's loss began Spain's long decline.

Don Diego spent his time interviewing hundreds of elderly Conquest survivors, collecting tales from people who had witnessed the birth of New World and Old. An ex-conquistador he talked to lay on a *petate*, hands and feet swollen useless, recalling the Aztec capital the morning he saw it first—skyline of turret and watchtower, eagles and jaguars painted on stucco. A hundred-year-old Aztec recalled the night a maguey plant with face and hands came to him in a dream. The next day, don Diego wrote, the superstitious fool threw up an altar to that plant.

*　　*　　*　　*　　*

In a windowless office, deep in the Washington State Employment Security Complex, Jesús Fuentes's hat revolved in his hands. He studied it, wide brim, tassel. A court-appointed interpreter kept murmuring that the state wanted its money back. A judge was insisting that Jesús return some $2,000 he had received in unemployment compensation. Documents in a folder suggested that Jesús had sworn to statements less than truthful. By now the judge was asking whether Jesús wanted an attorney.

Jesús studied the floor. He measured his words, and then allowed that he was little used to appearing in circumstances such as these. One was a working man after all. One maintained a certain standard of living for one's family. Surely a gentleman as worldly as the judge could see that before him, in Jesús—who was of course the judge's humble servant—the judge had a fellow entirely out of his element. The judge shook his head like a diver emerging from underwater. Then he repeated himself. Did Mr. Fuentes understand that he had the right to an attorney?

Jesús barely paused for breath. It was that infernal machine that had sent him those checks. He rolled his eyes. How could one be guilty if a machine had made an error? "You'll get a chance to testify," the judge muttered. "Now I need to know whether you want an attorney. Please answer yes or no." But by now, Jesús hit full stride. "When machines rule our lives," he wagged one finger, "we scarcely deserve to be called men and women. Far better it were to pluck those ignoble computers from where they sat and cast them as far as our strength permitted, no?"

So the interpreter called timeout. And then told Jesús that he probably did want a lawyer, and the judge gave him a month to get one. Out on the sidewalk, Jesús savored what seemed to him a clear-cut victory. Didn't the interpreter think Jesús handled that judge pretty well? Then an afterthought hit him, and he blinked. All things were in God's hands, *ni más ni menos*.

❋   ❋   ❋   ❋   ❋

This was the Yakima Valley and the 1990s after all. Seventh-day Adventists, Jehovah's Witnesses, Charismatics speaking in tongues, Mormon missionaries in neckties—any trailer court was full of worship alternatives. Maybe most mexicanos still paid lip service to the faith they brought from The Other Side. But clearly it was something very different that kept them alive. Their survival here owed to equilibrium of spirit, a resilience that seeped through topics otherwise too painful or boring for words. If mexicano belief at the end of the twentieth century tripped over abject devotions—La Guadalupana, La Familia, La Patria—it ended by recovering its balance, only to seem grotesque and lovely, ludicrous and wise.

Like electric current through copper, mexicano belief moved through a certain medium. Call it a prevailing persuasion, a collective hunch—in even the most sincere expression of Mexican belief, a kind of wry detachment crackled, a down-at-the-heels wit. Call it mexicano misgivings about this world. Maybe no more than a diction shift or play on words, and rarely worth repeating, it didn't translate at all, but so what?

Maybe mexicano belief did seem, to the Anglo ear, to be all tone of voice, one wacky episode after another. Anglos were forever saying that mexicano life preserved the pace of interpersonal ceremony, of greetings and farewells, phrases to wish that someone's meal or voyage went well. So what if mexicano fascination with fate sounded, to gringo ears, a bit tinny? Let them call it *stoicism*. Surviving alongside the plushest realm the earth had ever known really *did* call for something like stoicism.

Mexicano belief was hard to distinguish from mexicano humor, which made for uncanny effects. The mixed note that resulted came, in its purest form, from *los ancianos*, the elderly, those acrobats of tone and perspective. The long grind of their lives left behind only a tired smile, understatement, deadpan hyperbole. Because they barely needed speech, each trope flew into place with a couple of words. Even children recognized an elderly tone of voice. It didn't make fun of, or feel sorry for. It hit an in-between note. It was the crisp, anonymous feel of old sayings, *dichos*, *refranes*. That tone of voice bracketed the don or doña with self-awareness, and cast a penumbra the envy of all who suspected that life was really made out of cruel mirth.

❧   ❧   ❧   ❧   ❧

Don Diego was writing a handbook. He meant to portray the native belief system—in details as vivid as the faithful would confide to him—the better to eradicate any practice not appropriate to Holy

Mother Church. He had to. These *inditos* were hopeless backsliders. Don Diego winced to learn that markets sold more dog meat than beef, as eating dog meat was part of the Old Gods' worship. Often, their priests snatched up some couple that he had married and hustled them off and married them pagan-style.

One chilly Sunday morning as don Diego trudged to Mass, he met an elderly man, firewood roped to his back, tottering toward the public market. "How much will you get for your wood?" the don asked. "One *real*." "Then take this *real* and go home and make a fire and get yourself warm. Go ahead. It's a gift." Naturally, when he later saw the same senior citizen in the market vending the very same firewood, don Diego hit the ceiling. He accused the guy of slinking off to market to buy supplies for some pagan ceremony. But no, the old fellow offered to return the coin, and swore he merely had his heart set on getting that wood to market. Of his faith in God and Holy Mother Church, he spoke with an aplomb that don Diego admired, and wanted to test, but didn't dare. "No," he wrote, "I left him there. I make these little observations only to show the rigor with which people here protect their beliefs."

❋　　❋　　❋　　❋　　❋

Jesús and his wife wintered every year in their hometown in Michoacán. Like thousands of other couples drawn north by conditions of soil and climate, then south by family ties, they drove the very same three thousand miles, valley by valley, twice a year. Jesús simply pointed the pickup like a TV remote control and, *zas*, a century and a half of history came and went across their windshield.

They went back to a ranchito, an antique way of life, a scrap of the nineteenth century held in place by stubbornness and poverty. Cobblestones, tile roof, it was picturesque as hell. Nopal cactus ten feet tall, stone fences, it made for an isolation so dense that cowboys still enlivened a pail of fresh milk with Swiss Miss and grain alcohol in the morning, and flat-footed the thing, and rode off to work all day. But what *did* they call that beverage? Jesús had to think. Nowadays people called it a *toro prieto*. Though Jesús could remember his grandfather saying that, back in the 1890s, people called it a *palomillo*.

It was in the time of Jesús's grandfather that Mexican Central Plateau life underwent a trauma. Everybody in Michoacán agreed with that. Historically, it resembled the trauma Yakima County underwent when the Northern Pacific arrived, providing an outlet for Columbia Plateau wheat. The twentieth century caught up with Michoacán when private interests bought miles of swampland and drained it. Out of nowhere appeared guys who talked like books. They cleared their throats, reached in a paper bag that had writing on it, and extracted the twentieth century in the form of a new kind of seed corn. When they stuck that stuff in the ground, it yielded fat, heavy kernels that right away became what people wanted.

With so much acreage in corn, with tractors eliminating the need for labor, country boys like Jesús's grandfather wandered off to the United States to work in railroad construction. The migrant flow kept swelling during the twenties, only to shrink with massive deportations during the Great Depression. But it was the Bracero Program, during the 1940s, which truly began the modern era of mexicano life in the U.S. Northwest. Whole trainloads of men journeyed up from Mexico City to harvest crops.

And yet, despite the high wages, mexicanos never really trusted life in the north. From one of the early bracero trains—legend has it—half the passengers emptied out in Irapuato because of a rumor: the gringos meant to get them across the border, and then send them off to the front in World War II. After the war millions of young men rode trains north without even paying. Traveling fly-style they called it. The famous comedian Cantinflas—according to another legend—wanted to give the Mexican government two million pesos to let those poor people alone.

❋　　❋　　❋　　❋　　❋

When don Diego became old, he felt shortchanged. He grew a halo of ambivalence. The Old Gods thrived, and Holy Mother Church remained as oblivious as ever. The Old Gods even survived intact on the stone blocks that Spaniards tore out of native temples, then mortared back in place in the form of nunneries and schools. Where Indian kids conjugated Spanish verbs, or the Brides of Christ snored with their hands folded, the Old Gods leered down at them. And only don Diego was paying attention. He wrote that the Conquest never would be over.

In 1580, at a chapel at the foot of Mt. Popocatépetl, sacred to the Old Gods, he attended the Mass of Pentecost. It happened on that particular year to coincide with the Feast of Tezcatlipoca, the Aztec god with the most seniority. The courtyard was packed. Don Diego took a deep breath and kept his eyes on the ground. But even so he noticed the faithful were brandishing not candles but the flowered wands of Tezcatlipoca. Don Diego watched the priest performing the Mass lead them off in solemn cortege. I see these things, he wrote, but I keep quiet. He picked up a flowered wand. He got in line.

❊   ❊   ❊   ❊   ❊

The waiting room door flew open. And in rushed Jesús's wife, Cuca. Towing Epigmenio, their oldest boy, by the sleeve, she looked around. Was this the place to get her kid a driver's license? Yes, but it would be a while. So Cuca took a number and sat down. Then she started chatting with the interpreter—how Epi needed to marry a *gringuita*, one just pretty enough that he could endure the five years it took to get working papers. The *mexicanitas* hereabouts wouldn't sleep with him anyway.

A slender good-looking kid of sixteen, shrewd and ambitious, Epi had a second-grade education. He detested field work, and meant to become a court interpreter. Hands shoved in pockets, he walked up to the desk when they called his number. Clipboard in hand, a young examiner went out the door. She circled the car, flipped her ponytail, and climbed in.

Cuca continued chatting. She needed someone to listen to a small triumph in her life. Cuca was learning how to control her temper. She and the eight other mexicanas cleaning rooms at a local motel had been reprimanded for arguing. For coming to blows even. The supervisor scolded everybody, but said that she was keeping an eye on Cuca in particular. But not now. Because, well—Cuca pulled on a long gray braid, choosing her words. Last Saturday at work, when a certain woman kept dissing her, *puras faltas de respeto*, Cuca began considering her options. She had, right there on her room-cleaning cart, the bottled water you need to fetch a person upside. But guess what Cuca did? Fists clenched so hard she couldn't breathe, Cuca merely smiled and said, "Look you fucking little whore, leave me alone."

The examiner lady interrupted. Cuca was ready to say pardon her language but no, the woman was beaming at Epi, handing him his license. Cuca and Epi stood there grinning at his *foto* grinning back at them, shirtfront unbuttoned, gold ring in left ear.

❅   ❅   ❅   ❅   ❅

Youngsters Epi's age always found work. They set out nailing pallets or pruning apple trees, and started saving money for a car. Before long they were collecting traffic citations: driving without a license, no registration, no insurance. Then they showed up in court before the judge, a woman of middle age, designer glasses and gray hair, white blouse and navy jacket. She always began by describing, slowly, what an arraignment was. Phrases four, five words long. Pausing for the certified interpreter.

At least they called it *interpretation*. But how could anyone really interpret exactly what José María meant the morning he said that yes he wanted a court-appointed attorney alright, but he also wanted to plead guilty. And later another guy admitted that sure he was driving without a license. But he wanted her honor to know that he took off work and went and applied, and *los muy carajos* wouldn't *give* him a license, OK? What was the interpreter going to say?

Moments like those took over. More than one interpreter winced as the classic mexicano excuses stepped forward, and one by one fell flat. It was like watching a species die out! Arguments beveled by generations of deals cut between traffic cop and driver, defendant and judge—truly authentic material all, *pues*, no interpreter could save them. All that folk art wilted. On the unforgiving planks of English, Mexican rhetoric flopped and wheezed and expired.

✿   ✿   ✿   ✿   ✿

Diego Durán's book never saw print until three centuries after his death. By then, of course, the syncretism it meant to counteract had seeped through Holy Mother Church. And yet, if all of don Diego's surveillance yielded only a quaint set of field notes, his thinking survived at a subtler depth. Jesús Fuentes and family inherited all of the don's taste for ambivalence, for feelings framed with resistance and resignation. Neither Jesús nor his family ever heard of him, of course. But don Diego, let us say, left them not his doctrines but his attitude— not the same old dogma blurred by syncretism, but rather a perspective triggered by it, captive to it. Call it fly-style faith. It travels light.

Nobody knows when or where such a faith originated. But don't we see it already in the death of St. Lawrence, a third-century deacon? At least by the time, late in his life, when Lawrence assembled the Roman poor, it must have been second nature to him. Otherwise, why would he invite a Roman prefect to view what Lawrence promised—with a straight face—would be the Treasures of the Church? "And just where *are* the Treasures?" the prefect snapped. When Lawrence nodded at that gaggle of folk, barefoot and smelly, uncombed and hungry, the prefect was beside himself. He promptly had poor Lawrence burned alive.

St. Ambrose's biography records that Lawrence was seared on a gridiron like meat. It was a martyrdom surely meant to distract attention from what the likes of Diego Durán and the Fuentes family would notice in Lawrence's gesture forever after. In nodding at the poor, St. Lawrence confessed his own wry detachment. He admitted loving an imperfect world because of, not despite, the way it simply wouldn't live up to anybody's ideal version of it.

II   Figures of Speech

5 Chain Letter

It was in Spanish, handwritten, sentences uphill with *b* in place of *v*, *s* instead of *c*. In that mechanical tone that country folk strike when imitating official documents, it claimed to be a letter from the Virgin of Guadalupe. And the instructions were straightforward: make twenty-four copies and distribute them in thirteen days. So there I was, with a letter from La Virgen in my hand. *Pués, allí muere.*

Two weeks later, having made and handed out twenty-four copies, I picked up my buddy José and went to 7 a.m. Mass. It was December 12: exactly 475 years before, an ordinary guy named Juan Diego, finally granted an audience, flipped open his ragged cloak and spilled snow and Castillian roses on a bishop's floor.

The church José and I attended, by the way, was Episcopalian, but so what? This bishop had driven over from Spokane to celebrate a mass for La Virgen de Guadalupe. Her reproduction stood before the altar. The streamers of crepe paper at her feet were red and green and white, the colors of the Mexican flag.

The farmworker family in front of us had brought an eight-year-old son to be baptized today. They had the kid decked out in white shirt and a suit cut down to fit him. Tie fiercely knotted, he held the candle they gave him, staring into the flame, blinking, nodding. Beside him sat his father: a guy with thinning hair reading the Lord's Prayer in a clear, even voice. Behind us sat men in Levi's and denim jackets and boots and baseball caps, women in polyester slacks or cotton dresses, plus two teenage girls with new permanents.

While the bishop fought hard with the Spanish he had to pronounce, and the word *misericordia* derailed him, babies hummed and fussed in the background. A two-year-old crawled down the aisle in a satin dress and a baseball cap. When the bishop explained that to take Communion a person needn't have confessed, the kid to be baptized wisecracked—albeit in a stage whisper—that local folks had sinned so much the bishop wouldn't have time to confess them all.

We sat in the choir room after Mass, nibbling beef tamales, sipping coffee or *atole*. I mentioned in passing that the Virgin seemed, in this reproduction, fairer of complexion than I remembered; the mother of the baptized kid winked and whispered that the gringos maybe had dabbed a bit of makeup on her.

When José and I were leaving he asked, in that perfectly unaccented Arizona English of his, where he should put the cornhusks from the tamales. One of the Anglo ladies in aprons looked up. She saw this great big brown guy standing there with a handful of husks, and got flustered, and her mind did a backflip. Articulating broadly, drawing out huge gestures, she indicated the garbage went right *heeeeere*. In the *waaaaaste* basket.

❊   ❊   ❊   ❊   ❊

A lot is written about mexicano immigrants, and much of it makes them look like effigies, placeholders arranged to illustrate some argument. The people I know are very different, not surprisingly, both from any stereotype and from each other. My friends long ago internalized the U.S.–Mexican border by crossing it: a street full of potholes and skinny dogs, to a McDonald's drive-through lane and a freeway cloverleaf.

Unpredictable, self-contradictory even, my friends zip through each other's lives, and through mine, drawn by a propeller-blur of feelings, tough and funny and sad and sly, exuberant and reserved, frolicsome and stern. When things get tight, a kind of lyric despair flies through what they say, a stoical whimsy that leaves an illiterate kid on an apple ladder sounding like Marcus Aurelius.

"¿Tú qué eres, nopal o bolillo?" a kid asked the other day in a high school class I visited. He wanted to know which side of that border I myself came from. With two answers being possible, and neither one of them the truth, I told him how the last time I walked across the border two Chicano college professors went ahead of me in line. Speaking unaccented English, they slid through the turnstile and up to the INS agent on duty. Asking in a cheerful way about their citizenship, the agent waved them on, nodding.

Meanwhile, I myself was in a conversation in Spanish with an elderly woman, right behind me in line, who happened to come from a village in Chihuahua where my car broke down one weekend years before. Finally, when I stood before the agent, he squinted and asked in Spanish where I was born. "Nací en los Estados Unidos," I replied. "¿Y precisamente dónde nació Ud.?" he persisted. "Pos' yo nací en Spraangfeel, Missuhrah, ol' buddy." The agent flinched and laughed. The student said OK and changed the subject.

❃   ❃   ❃   ❃   ❃

Michoacán and the whole Mexican Central Plateau train, on the twenty-first century Inland Empire, a stream of mexicano lives so endless you recall how Spanish life was projected—five centuries ago, and far more fiercely—onto the Mexican Central Plateau. By 1531 the conquering, Christianizing Spaniards were wrecking pyramids, topping off the rubble with churches. The Aztecs by now—witnessing the annihilation of everything they worshiped, from temple to breastplate to causeway—lay around dying of fevers they'd never felt before. It was during this time that the peasant Juan Diego, passing Tepeyac hill one night, heard La Virgen say she wanted a shrine built right where she stood. By the time Juan finally faced the bishop after seven days of entreaties, her features imbued the fibers of his cloak. And her features were brown. She was a *morenita*.

Her skin color says worlds about the Spanish Conquest, the desperation of a people suddenly aware their skin was brown. To this day, people crawl on their knees to visit that cloak. Some days the sidewalk is littered with worn-out basketball knee-pads.

Her Aztec worshipers certainly needed all the forgiveness she could manage, given their compulsive way of blaming themselves for the Conquest, or at least their habit of placing the blame on one of their own. The person they blamed, another morenita, comes to us under the name La Malinche. That "most excellent companion of Cortez," chronicler Bernal Diaz de Castillo calls her. She served Cortez as interpreter and guide, and went to bed with him. Doña Marina, the Spaniards called her. Tradition blames the whole Conquest on her. They say La Malinche rejected her people for strangers who in turn rejected her. To this day to be called a *malinchista* means that you've adopted foreign ways.

    ❋   ❋   ❋   ❋   ❋

La Malinche and La Virgen: while they form the border between accusation and pardon, self-blame and self-forgiveness, they register the gravitational tug of a third morenita. People call her La Llorona. People identify her as an Aztec woman who fell in love with a Spaniard of noble birth, then bore him several children, only to see his parents call him back to Spain to marry the woman they had selected for him. When he told her he meant for their children to receive a proper Spanish upbringing, she drowned them. Her punishment was forever to wander around bodies of water hunting her children.

What a trio! La Malinche accumulates in your life, disguised as foreign influence, while from birth to the very last Hail Mary your mouth emits, you count on La Virgen's forgiveness. But La Llorona is very different. She confronts, and defies.

Say a young man comes lurching down a sidewalk after a night of celebration. He starts to flirt with a well-dressed female figure. In Spanish-speaking countries, the situation isn't hard to read: *mujer sola, va a ser puta o fea*; a woman by herself at night is bound to be either a whore or ugly. When the object of his flirtation withdraws, answering in monosyllables, he pursues until she turns, and he sees her fleshless skull. The *susto*, or fright, is said to cure a fellow of keeping late hours, of drinking and hustling women.

La Llorona shows up in hundreds of versions. She can be an Indian from the early years of the Conquest, or a campesina from twenty years ago. She may have drowned two children or three, or maybe only one. Once I even heard of her killing them with an obsidian knife, Aztec fashion. Whatever else, her anger is a counterweight to Guadalupe's forgiveness, so impersonal that it extends even to those who wrong her children. La Llorona forgives nothing. She loves her children too much to see them inhabit a world that hates them because of their color. Anywhere water collects, La Llorona haunts it like surface tension. La Malinche, meanwhile, makes do. Let the other two continue accusing and forgiving, La Malinche seems to say. She slips into history without a ripple. A great deal of Mexican history, however, depends on how you answer one question. Which of the three nurtures her children best?

History seems to favor La Malinche, who snuffs her resentment, not her children, while rejecting La Guadalupana's example of chastity as well. Malinche pretty clearly goes to bed with a guy to survive the greatest human die-off in the planet's history. A parody of the Mexican national anthem reminds us: *México tiene soldado en cada hijo de la chingada*. It is from La Malinche that mexicanos and mexicanas descend.

❖   ❖   ❖   ❖   ❖

La Virgen and La Malinche and La Llorona form a three-dimensional view, one that mestizo people communicate with double takes and shrugs. To follow the three at work in daily life is to backtrack and plunge, zigzag and cut corners, to superimpose bits of discontinuous action—while, for example, neighbor Ramón is relating his scrape with the law, heavy-lidded eyes flashing from indignation to self-ridicule.

He slapped his wife and was arrested one Sunday night. How'd that happen? He got back from a 1,200-mile trip to Fresno to straighten out his wife's brother's working papers. The brother-in-law didn't know how to drive a standard transmission, though, so Ramón logged 2,400 miles round trip. In seventy-two hours. Forearms trembling, fingers stiff, he sat down that Sunday night in his kitchen, only to learn that his oldest boy had just driven off in the family car. Even though the kid had no license. Like his older sisters—twenty-one and twenty-three, the two of them—he was staying out all night with friends, sleeping till noon.

Ramón downed a couple of beers, and thought. After hearing his wife announce for the umpteenth time that their son was grown, and couldn't be denied use of the car, Ramón slapped her. Except that maybe he didn't. Even the wife, by the next morning, wasn't sure what happened. The six-year-old son, scared, had dialed 911. Ramón got out of jail because I offered him a place to stay.

And our three female figures. What role did they play? They were three dimensions of his state of mind, three backhand nuances I heard. True, if other figures nuanced my thinking, I might have heard other dimensions instead. But other figures don't nuance my thinking: I heard remorse and resentment ascending to a forgiveness so steep it tipped into new remorse, new resentment. By Friday, Ramón knew he'd be able to see his wife and kids on Monday. All he needed to do was survive the weekend. Early Monday morning, his wife phoned in tears. Ramón was in jail again, a DWI this time, plus vehicular assault, hit-and-run, and violating the court's no-contact order. He could be released, but only into an alcohol treatment program. Which meant he'd have to be interviewed by Social Services. So, within two weeks, if their quota wasn't full, they might be able to work him in, they told me and then hung up.

La vida no vale nada. An old song reassures us, life is worth nothing at all. It is a notion derived in equal parts from Pedro Infante and Marcus Aurelius: *no vale nada la vida.* An invitation to delight in how utterly worthless life is! No matter how many miles you lug that apple ladder, some Monday morning will reduce you to nothing but song lyrics.

❄   ❄   ❄   ❄   ❄

La vida no vale nada alludes to the hairline-fracture despair that runs through much of mexicano life. It teaches detachment. In the famous interviews Manuel Gamio conducted in 1926–27, poor people train the calm of a dead Roman emperor on their grief. Before the Revolution even ended, one guy, deserting the Villistas, hopped a train to the border and found work on a street-paving crew. His interview recalls moonlit battles, foaming horses, and ditches full of dead Yaquis. A fellow who deserted the ranks of Carranza remembers Villa's round shoulders and broad head and fierce look.

Was life worth more after the Mexican Revolution? Ask the mother—flat nose, pockmarked—who begs with her eighteen-month-old kid in a plaza in Ciudad Juárez, or ask her husband, around the corner, selling birdcages. Or the house servant who saved his money and started a corner store, only to be kidnapped by Villistas. Escaping to El Paso, he worked in different railroad camps, drifting to the cement plants in L.A., then to Kansas, Oklahoma, and wound up running drills in Miami, Arizona.

Reared in the house of the bishop of Sonora, a sculptor of santos—adept at carving wood, marble or chalk—reads only Mexican newspapers. Even though he lives in Chicago, selling tiny likenesses of La Guadalupana and Francisco Madero, he refuses to learn English. He's got plans to go back, after all.

Mexicanas and mexicanos find work, and foremen fill the air with "sanavaviches" and "gardemes." For each day we put in crossing this country, somebody tells Gamio, we love our own country more. The bolillos do what they want with us, another says, because we don't learn English. We sleep late Sundays, instead. Then we head for a pool hall, or a dance hall. The United States is a jail in disguise.

❋   ❋   ❋   ❋   ❋

Ramón got out. He slipped through the polished wood of a lawyer's desk, the buzz and thunk of security systems. Jurisdictions overlapped. When he left for a treatment center, I put him on a bus and shook his hand.

This morning, a month later, he's back—all wry tone and crooked grin. The counselors, he says, convinced him of one thing at least: all the problems he left would certainly be here waiting for him on his return. Plus other problems.

This morning his wife, Rocío, settles into her quilted jacket, and sighs good morning. She's beautiful in a rare, old-country way: classically curved Maya nose and large brown eyes, slender torso, nimble walk. She has the mix of warmth and reserve that characterizes country folk. She still, after all these years, addresses me as *Usted*. Like well-mannered country people, she covers her mouth when she laughs.

Rocío makes this story literal. Forms of forgiveness, shame, and revenge do run through her, of course. But mainly she's the same, frazzled, forty-year-old person who microwaved pizza last night, before heading off to the Laundromat. Today her clear-eyed resignation says it all: that even though life here is conducted in English, and men and women eat at the same table, and no one says *salud* when you sneeze, certain figures are recognizable.

This morning Ramón and I are driving Rocío to work. We pass jack-o'-lanterns shattered in the street. Corn stalks decorate porches, and M&M's crunch under our tires, because last night was Halloween, that weirdest of all bolillo holidays. Once every twelve months, kids scramble door to door for candy—oh what fleeting stuff the body is made of!—and next morning the skeleton suits get tucked away for another year.

Not so on The Other Side. In Guerrero, Rocío recalls, whole families trek out to graveyards to picnic around the tomb of a loved one. Either that or an altar in the living room holds the favorite food of the departed. Maybe a trail of yellow petals leads from the graveyard gate to the front door. At least, it used to be that way. She remembers when men and boys went house to house, serenading the souls of the dead. Parents touched off firecrackers and rockets to attract dead children home for a visit.

What's the point? That the bolillos disguise death with candy and costumes? That early-November, low-angle light shrink-wraps color and feeling? People get used to it in time. Before long Rocío will have their two little boys made up as vampires prowling a local mall with candy sacks at the ready.

Rocío recalls how, in her village in Guerrero in the sierra, people remembered the dead that no one else would remember by leaving a candle to blink all night in their doorway. Beside it they left a scrap of bread and a cup of cocoa. For the length of a blink, there it is: Mexican Central Plateau life, pebbles balanced on the arms of cemetery crosses, a plastic bouquet in a coffee can, a burlap sack leaking the yellow *flor de muerto* that people heap on graves.

Rocío grins and says so long. She opens a motel service entrance door to put in eight hours fluffing pillows and scrubbing toilets.

❈   ❈   ❈   ❈   ❈

On either side of La Virgen, like wings, La Llorona and La Malinche hover. They interlock down to the last nuance. They comment on each other with the strangled eloquence of facts. Only La Virgen, of course, receives ecclesiastical recognition. And yet, while time edges La Virgen with two very different borders of growth—an appetite for justice, an aptitude for betrayal—all three hint at one truth. La raza's hard-won detachment owes to apparitions and counter-apparitions that crowd people's thinking.

Devotion to La Virgen spread like a chain letter through the New World. She was named Queen of this Hemisphere only 18 years after Juan flipped open his cloak. But right from the start she carried her parenthetical selves, the numinous pair who remind us that what we worship is superimposition.

6　Anecdotes and Proverbs

For the same reasons other people collect folk masks or woven goods, I collect mexicano immigrant anecdotes, tales that form the world my neighbors live in. My taste for such material even has me accepting collect phone calls from strangers.

After the night I agreed to run a message down the road to a phone-less neighbor—her cousin called, broken down one hundred miles out in the sagebrush—word got around. By now those who call collect are friends of friends, hardworking, responsible folk who need to borrow a quick fifty, or hide a car for a few days, people every bit as honest as their circumstances let them be, and frequently a lot more so. Anyhow, I wind up accepting calls from guys named El Güero and El Cholo, El Pollo and El Pajarito, from señoras named Chole and Cuca, Mago and Mema.

It isn't that I can't say no. Far from it. I accept their calls in the same spirit in which an antique-dealer friend of mine attends an estate sale: out of respect for the law of averages. My own twitchy curiosity demands to know what anecdote tugs on the other end of that phone line.

My neighbors live in a news shadow, a corner of Columbia Plateau desert as yet unreached by Spanish-speaking media. Pretty much ignored by English-language newspapers and TV, with no source of "reliable reportage," they lead an existence free of "facts," with no agreed-upon limits. They live in a world they patch together from freeway scuttlebutt, shopping mall innuendo, Laundromat hearsay. And what effect does the lack of hard data have on the information they exchange? Opposite versions of the same event co-exist. People shrug a lot. The buzz and rumble of skillful, uninhibited rumor-mongering produces stories explained by other stories, tales taken at face value—which in turn makes for its own kind of coverage.

❀   ❀   ❀   ❀   ❀

I do a lot of double takes at what my neighbors infer from any anecdote, let alone the ones they tell each other. The young, especially, amaze me with the conclusions they can draw. Take for example the summer my buddy Lowell, a minister, suggested I round up a dozen mexicano kids who were running loose. While their parents were putting in twelve-hour shifts at the local freezer plant, those little guys needed supervision. How about if I brought them to Bible School? The church would provide workbooks in Spanish.

That was how, one Thursday morning in July, I faced two rows of squirming ten-year-olds. The scripture for the day was from Luke: Joseph and Mary taking young Jesus to Jerusalem, where he winds up instructing the rabbis. We took turns reading the story aloud. "What do we learn from the story?" I asked, like it said to in the Teacher's Manual. "What does the ending show us about the Lord?" I waited, like it said to, for an answer.

And *zas* out of his chair came Paco, a redheaded kid with a piercing voice and heavy freckles, good-hearted but ornery, inveterate burper during solemn moments, a fellow much given to peeking up skirts and making prank telephone calls. Paco said that, frankly, he thought my question was pointless. He saw a larger issue here. "¿Qué clase de papás serán?" he waved one stubby finger. "What kind of parents were Mary and Joseph? Hadn't they left their only son, by accident, in Jerusalem? Didn't even notice he was gone till the next day!"

"They want us to discuss what the story shows about Jesus," I countered. I was supervising, after all. "Of course they do," Paco's voice hit triumph range. "Anybody at all could see the story was about bad parents," he hissed, "people who pay no attention to their kids." By now other boys and girls were elbowing each other, nodding, and I was whipped. Hadn't done my homework. Though even if I had, so what? The topic under discussion was learning from children, right?

❊   ❊   ❊   ❊   ❊

The kind of anecdote my neighbors trade blends the ad-libbed and the scripted, giving off never-quite-identifiable signals. It quivers like a biopsy plucked from a hyperactive universe. Don't confuse such anecdotes with *set pieces*, the straightforward stuff that oral historians collect, narratives that march from beginning to middle to end. My neighbors' anecdotes frequently limp off, incomplete.

Like its fraternal twin the proverb—another mixed-feelings vehicle—my neighbors' type of anecdote often radiates opposite meanings. Anecdote and proverb both collect in cracks between grief and pride, desire and disgust, off-key or off-color, often plain pointless. Either one can be heard as an *indirecta*, a veiled disrespect, a deadpan cheekiness. Furthermore, each can be freestanding—neither uttered nor heard as a simple illustration of something under discussion. Neither one even has to present an exception which proves a rule. The proverb or anecdote can always claim non sequitur status.

❊   ❊   ❊   ❊   ❊

Paco's home life spliced different scenes of childhood slipping away. One night that summer his mother—my down-the-road neighbor—lined her children up in the living room. Said she herself never had a childhood, *hijos de su puta madre*. Said she meant to smoke crank and drink beer as much as she goddam wanted.

By dawn she's prowling an alley in pursuit of a dime bag. Locked in the bathroom, she holds a lighter under a scrap of tinfoil. She puts a rolled dollar bill to her nose, and feels better. She opens a beer, puts on a cassette. One of those long *corridos* from Sinaloa begins twanging, the kind where only resisting authority makes a man or woman worth singing about. She giggles that nowadays she does her resisting with tinfoil.

Now imagine her talking to an empty chair, a skillet crusted with beans, puckered lime slices on the table. A tortilla curls under her chair like a cat. She looks at her confirmation foto stuck on the wall with a Band-Aid, and weeps at what guys used to fall in love with.

❈   ❈   ❈   ❈   ❈

Nazareth lies seventy miles from Jerusalem, by the way, and in photos the landscape resembles the view that lies out our Methodist sanctuary window that morning. Scrubby, dry hills dipping and drooping, then horizon. Imagine the hardship it was for Jesus's family to celebrate Passover in Jerusalem. Afterward, Joseph and Mary did put in three days hunting their son. And yet I have to agree with Paco. The parenting skills seem laughable.

Trying to research that passage in Luke, I hit Google and came up with Biblical commentator David Guzik, a fellow who insists that scripture is autonomous. "There isn't anything we need to know," he writes, "except what we are told by the Holy Spirit in the Word." He dismisses any effort to understand the behavior of Jesus's parents. The fact that we can't answer objections like Paco's, he insists, merely indicates how wrongheaded the thinking behind them is. To consider the parenting skills of Mary and Joseph—to think, in general, that scripture records the deeds of flawed and funky people—encourages not faith but superstition, Guzik argues, reverence too flimsy for truly God-fearing folk.

Guzik insists that thinking like that of Paco characterizes the "so-called Infancy Gospels," anecdotes meant to satisfy idle curiosity about Jesus's life, full of miracles he calls "spectacular and silly." He characterizes those Gospels as gawky, tinny, meretricious.

Intrigued, I looked at the Childhood Gospels of Thomas the Israelite, and found a Christ Child as feisty as Paco, and much more lethal. One Sabbath, while playing, molding toy birds out of clay, He ordered a little brook to form puddles, and it did. When a passerby scolded Him for profaning the Sabbath, and broke up His puddles with a willow branch, Jesus shriveled the fool in his tracks. Then He clapped His hands and the birds flew off.

Later, He healed a severed foot with His touch, and humiliated two different scholars who tried to teach Him the alphabet. When He broke His mother's pitcher at a well, He carried water home in His cloak. Accused of pushing a playmate out the window of a tall building, Jesus leaped to the ground, saucy and indignant, and resurrected the kid on the spot. Other Childhood Gospels have Him speaking from the manger, and healing people by sprinkling them with His bathwater.

Scholars do remind us that all kinds of anecdotes crowded into Jesus's biography—pagan diversions, less-than-holy close-ups—until the early church fathers, by banishing such stuff from the canon, exercised the authority that still rings in Guzik's voice.

Meanwhile, it bothers my neighbors not at all that anecdotes thrive beyond the authority exercised by church fathers—or by the *New York Times*, for that matter. It is the nature of anecdotes to go through endless retelling and variation. No one gets worked up, down at the freezer plant, over some kid wowing a bunch of rabbis.

✳   ✳   ✳   ✳   ✳

Think what it feels like to limp out a side door after a twelve-hour shift, doffing a hairnet, fingertips wrinkled from all that steam. Produced by years of anecdotes and counter-anecdotes, by life rounded off to the nearest attitude, my friends' feelings about their children find expression in a proverb. "No saben lo que es amar a Dios," they tell each other. "No saben lo que es amar a Dios en tierra de indios." Literally referring to the difficulty of loving God in Indian country, the proverb alludes by extension to adapting to life in a foreign land. As proverbs go, it is close to being Mexican Immigrant Motto #1.

Loving God in Indian country! The idea recalls that handful of Spanish missionaries received by maybe twenty million native folk, speaking perhaps one thousand different languages. Those numbers are the guesswork of historians, of course, and every bit as approximate as estimates by those same historians whether it was eighty or ninety or ninety-five percent of those who did the receiving that died of fevers and bleeding and pustules we barely can diagnose even today.

❊   ❊   ❊   ❊   ❊

Fifteen years after our Bible School dialogue, Paco is a tall, good-looking young man—he and I now nod hello in parking lots. He drives a sanded, repainted Camaro convertible. God knows how he afforded that stereo system audible half a mile away, but of course he had to have it. From top-end stereo systems, after all, guys Paco's age absorb heroic events in the form of *narcocorridos*—folk ballads set in Sinaloa or in the states that border Texas. At stop lights, you hear lyrics highlighting the deeds of drug runners, *los contrabandistas*. "My voice is worn out from singing of Pablo Acosta," the lyrics fly from Paco's great big speakers,

> but guys who play with fire get burned
> and he was the czar of traffickers.
> Wanna know where to send flowers for
> this *chicanito* who gave to the poor?
> They dug a hole by the Rio Grande
> on the Chihuahua side. They piled
> a bunch of dirt on him
> and drove a cross in it like a nail.

❊   ❊   ❊   ❊   ❊

Fifteen years go by, and one morning Paco's mother—clean and sober for ten of those years—drives a granddaughter to kindergarten one morning. It's the very first day of school. The door whooshes, and they enter. Paco's mother carries in one hand a letter in English. She pauses at a classroom door, catching the eye of a woman standing surrounded by little kids. Blonds and redheads. Freckles, braces. The minute that woman smiles, Paco's mother thrusts the letter and the granddaughter at her, pronouncing the granddaughter's name very slowly.

The teacher wears a microphone pinned to her lapel, and out of speakers on the ceiling, her voice falls on five little tables, each with five tiny chairs, with name tags and folders and pencils and crayons. The teacher waves Paco's mother inside for a visit. But when Paco's mother imagines how she'd look, perched on one of those tiny chairs, with one thick haunch in the air, a weird shame creeps over her. She beats it out a side door and into the parking lot.

Ten minutes of steering and blinking get her back to her living room: drab plaids and airy pastels, a sofa with wooden arms, beer-can-ringed, cigarette-scorched, beside it a velour lump with whiny springs. Beyond, a leatherette recliner lies paralyzed, mid-recline, as if it were baring its throat.

Seedy, yes, but her standard of living has risen. By now she enjoys a life of amenities held in place by willpower. This morning, however, she recalls a $50 bill she stashed last week in a Maseca bag. Like swallowed milk, the memory trails through her. Discretionary spending power, they call it.

❖   ❖   ❖   ❖   ❖

For every proverb that mentions God, another one refers to the devil. Maybe some predisposition toward balanced coverage is at work, an equal-time doctrine for the mexicano soul. Certainly people the age of Paco's mother rarely pass up a chance to remind people Paco's age of what is, they say, the single advantage of being middle-aged or elderly. "El diablo sí sabe más por viejo que por diablo," they say. The devil knows more because he is old than because he's the devil. Call it Mexican Immigrant Motto #2. Even in the world of narcocorridos, even in the life of Pablo Acosta—the proverb implies—age understands more than wickedness can invent.

Knowing by now that age always out-imagines wickedness, Paco's mother recalls that proverb this morning. Accumulation of anecdotes, she recalls, has taught her more than her own ugly urges ever did. And that's a moral too straightforward for even Paco to ignore.

Pablo's wickedness—she admits it!—made him so many zillions of dollars that he no doubt expected Jesus Himself to phone collect. And yet, look at photos of Pablo from right before he died. Notice something atrophied about the guy? That's what learning from children leads to! With his shirt half open, his Cartier watch, his wanted-poster eyes, Pablo looks like a kid's idealized version of a fifty-year-old man.

7   Corrido

. . . to find the archetypal image of Eve in the corrido in
various manifestations as "La Belle Dame sans Merci" (i.e.,
coquette and seductress), the disobedient mate or the traitor.

MARÍA HERRERA-SOBEK, *The Mexican Corrido*

Meche was meant to be the kind of woman guys knife each other over.
Her whole trailer court said so. Skinny, with big eyes and a chin dim-
ple, pouty lips. When she turned nine, they gave her mascara, a fingernail kit, eyeliner. But now she was twenty-four. And on this particular
night, she lay—hadn't even shaved her legs—bleeding half-naked in
an emergency room. With her face beaten shapeless, and three kids at
home asleep, her bloodstained brassiere and T-shirt in a corner. In her
head was something the doctor called a subdural hematoma.

Only a blunt instrument could have done what the X-rays revealed.
What happened? The doctor wanted to know, the interpreter kept
shouting in her ear. "¿M'ija, quién te hizo esto?" She shuddered,
sighed. Did she know what year it was? The doctor was shouting.
Both eyes puffed shut, lip split, her head lolled against a plastic neck
brace. She slumped and clenched, nipples erect.

The doctor talked slowly to control his voice. Probably, she was
going to die. Onto a dab of asphalt out back, a helicopter quivered
down. Doors flew open.

※　　※　　※　　※　　※

It all sounded like a corrido: (1) her body was very fine, and (2) it was
covered with blood. The whole trailer court agreed, however, that nobody wanted problems of the dishonored-father/jealous-husband variety. All of this was explosive stuff, material just waiting for corrido

lyrics to be imposed on it. A half-naked wife beat up? Who wouldn't recall ballads about gunfights, faithless women, and horses that die running.

After all, one corrido after another says it: *por no saberse tantear.* In the world of corridos, the people who get killed are those who disdain half-measures, who never learn the knack of slipping up on, easing into, people without talent for living inconspicuously. Corridos portray people taking the law into their own hands. A classic corrido community—argues John H. McDowell—sprouts in a climate of violence, of grievances that can't be resolved through legal channels.

❊   ❊   ❊   ❊   ❊

When they interviewed Meche's boyfriend Gustavo, yes, he drove her to the emergency room, and no, he didn't know what had happened to her. He stroked his jaw and thought.

Dry-eyed, calm, self-deprecating, a wiry guy with stubby fingers, pointed features, untamable hair, Gustavo grew up in backwoods Guerrero. He walked around with a certain awed glee that he was really here in el norte earning dollars. Back home, it was nothing but hitchhiking down the coast to cut cane, back to the hills to put in a crop. Everybody muttered about police and merchants and landowners: people who won't feed us, and won't let us die of hunger. Down at the bus depot, guys like Gustavo showed up with a change of clothing and headed north.

Gustavo was accustomed to being questioned by Guerrero's Preventive Police. Imagine three or four guys burning a stubble field, when Governor Figueroa's men drive up. To start the interrogation, they order the guys to dig a deep hole, then throw one in, and make the other two bury him. They drive their tinted-window van back and forth over the dirt and start the questioning.

But not here. Arrested once, Gustavo had seen a court-appointed attorney for fifteen minutes, and came out delirious with relief. Someone believed his alibi! After that, he was convinced the legal system was fair. A man could get along en el norte. Gustavo didn't so much as jaywalk.

Now he gave a resigned shiver and raised his T-shirt to let them check for signs of a fight. That blood smear on the side of his shoe came, he said, from when he lifted her into the car. In rushed a tall wide woman with henna hair and tiny features—Meche's mother, Estela—who glanced at her daughter, and then collapsed facedown on a gurney and howled. Her husband Candelario followed her into the room and buried his face in his hands. He said excuse him please. Needed to make a few phone calls. When he reappeared in ten minutes and whispered in his wife's ear, both stiffened and eyed the cop. "Have them detain the boyfriend," don Cande hissed.

✻   ✻   ✻   ✻   ✻

Don Cande favored huaraches woven from thick black ribbons of leather Michoacán-style, and a baseball cap with a grain mill logo faded off the crown. Not even the mouthiest teenager said anything to him. People whispered that don Cande killed a guy once on the Costa Chica. You noticed the way his blind eye aimed at you. It was the left eye, the one *curanderos* clear a sickroom with. Voice always silky quiet, the brim of his cap low, don Cande walked like a cat. A permanent grief held his face.

And yet even don Cande was drained by the time he got his wife out the hospital door, having awakened at 4 a.m. when the phone rang. Now he led his wife through a parking lot full of wet twigs and bird calls. He started his pickup and drove home, slapping at the steering wheel, dabbing his eyes.

He ate nothing. By that afternoon, brooding over a single beer in the cab of his truck in the driveway, Cande was conducting a hearing. In the corners of his mind it all accumulated: someone had punched out his daughter. So what if the police had her boyfriend. So what if the hospital said that she would live. If it was just about his own feelings, Cande could let the cops handle this *rollo*, but he had people observing him. He lived, in effect, in a tiny Mexican village, a couple thousand people from Michoacán and Guerrero—scattered among twenty thousand Anglos who barely noticed them. Wasn't every mexicano hereabouts waiting to see what Cande would do?

Cande and his wife had reared a pack of problem kids. Everybody agreed. In every apartment they rented, his family broke the hot-water heater, faucets, light switches. They stopped up the toilet and peed in the sink. No furniture survived. His kids gouged and whittled and stained their way into four-figure damage deposits. Till Cande one day said what the hell. He up and bought a double-wide way out in the sagebrush. It was the double-wide that he sat in front of now in the cab of his truck figuring out what to do. Cande had spent the afternoon thumbtacking tinfoil onto the corners of his house. The corners attracted woodpeckers, which in turn opened up thumb-size holes into the insulation and wiring. Now, in the afternoon sunlight, his house glittered, wholly woodpecker-proof. But inside the house, television cartoons shrieked and howled. So it was only in his truck, with the windows up, that Cande had room to wonder how he wound up here, in an irrigated desert, with a six-year-old son who answered him in English.

❀   ❀   ❀   ❀   ❀

Estela was on record. Buying this double-wide was a martyrdom. Just to meet the payments she had to scrub motel toilets all day, and then home to cook, do laundry, plus it was lonely out here. Here she was at the sink doing dishes at 10 p.m., while Cande sat out front, windows rolled up, terrified of his own feelings. He wouldn't look at her.

By now she barely knew Cande's feelings, aside from one quiver-chinned moment of trying to quote a poem someone had read at his father's funeral. Aside from his taste for pozole, and his regular tug on her nightgown, Cande invited her into his life not at all. Certainly it wasn't the Whole Other World she had expected when, at age sixteen, she tucked a change of clothes under his pickup front seat and headed off to el norte with him. For motives she no longer cared to think about, thank you.

Estela couldn't get rid of the image: of her daughter's face, nose broken, both eyes swollen shut, one cheek open to the bone. All that attention to detail! It looked like a lesson.

Estela's innards did an elevator dip, and she understood: her daughter's assailants were other women. Wives of guys with whom her daughter's name had been linked in the web of gossip and innuendo that life became every year when the freezer plant began that month-and-a-half of twelve-hour shifts, which people called La Pizca. A couple of tough tejanas had put a rock in a sock and worked on Meche's face. That was the simple truth. Estela knew it, and knew by the look on his face that Cande hunkered down out there in his pickup knew it.

Pinche Meche with a six-pack in a pickup in a parking lot after work, or phoning some guy's house and telling his wife to have him phone Meche, or dancing to car radio tunes under cottonwoods at lunch break. A Seattle hospital phoned last night to say they operated and she'd live. This morning Meche herself phoned and swore that she fell down a flight of stairs.

Tonight was the hard part. Better get it over with. Estela could get him out of that truck with a bowl of pozole, a red J.C. Penney housecoat, and a bit of fresh gossip about the neighbor lady. Estela dried dishes, and gazed at her *viejo*—kitchen window to windshield—while they made the decision. They would say that Meche had fallen down stairs.

❊   ❊   ❊   ❊   ❊

La Pizca was like no other part of the year. August and September, the freezer plant became so busy that nobody knew what day it was. The monotony of twelve-hour shifts left couples cheating on each other—in dreams, if not when awake—but everybody stayed connected like life-support to whatever marriage they were in the rest of the year.

Meche never had understood it: sometimes women too old to work joked that, late in life, it took them a night or two to realize they were sleeping alone. *Híjole*, what kind of existence was that? Meche lived for La Pizca.

On her first morning back in her own bed, Meche palmed three prescription Tylenols for the headache she anticipated. Then she remembered whom she had to talk to this morning and treated herself to a last codeine tablet tucked away months ago in a tampon box under the sink for the kids' earaches.

When a cop asked questions, Meche rolled her eyes and thought. She lowered her voice to a backcountry singsong and started in, tears spurting so hard that he drew a bandanna and handed it to her. But this was a different Meche, one who swallowed her s's like folk from the coast, and dabbed almond extract behind her ears, and knew she had damn little chance of being believed.

She spoke to that bandanna like a microphone. One night Gustavo didn't come home, and strange Anglo men attacked the house. The first empty beer bottle came through the window of the bedroom she and the kids were sleeping in. Voices from the dark yard kept shrieking Gustavo's name. She heard the windshield splinter on the car parked at her window. Imagine three children rigid in the middle of the floor, eyes screwed tight, screaming.

She even recalled how Gustavo came home later and got from under the sink a .22 rifle his cousin had lent him. He slipped in the little plastic clip and opened the kitchen door and closed it after him. When he came back he sat on the folding chair and gave her a funny smile. After that night nothing ever felt the same again.

Gustavo received three years for dealing cocaine.

❀   ❀   ❀   ❀   ❀

Fog collected on hay fields by October. The carrot line at the freezer plant creaked to a halt earlier each day, and people started kicking back. Those who would drive back to Texas were checking the air in their tires, spare clothing already in garbage bags tucked into camper corners. People about to winter in Michoacán already were talking of avocado and mamey, pineapple and *chirrimoya*. Everybody Meche knew by now was banged up in body and spirit.

From Meche's back window, she could watch the window where the neighbor lady stepped from a shower every evening to reposition a mustard plaster on the small of her back, where the husband drained a six-pack on the couch each morning at five when he got off. Body and spirit, people told themselves. Everyone had to work to keep the

spirit inside the body. The spirit wanted to fly off over yellow cot-
tonwood leaves into the fog. The body took a beating. But it was the
spirit that wanted out. It was the spirit.

❋   ❋   ❋   ❋   ❋

Cande and Estela? That autumn their feelings kept whizzing like plan-
ets around a star, all their grief and anger held in place by this particular bit of heartbreak. Then, other things happened. Neither of them
forgot. But each wished that time would bring the other a different set
of feelings. And one day it did.

Cande was the first to feel his emotions shift. One afternoon as
he was driving through the sagebrush, a tire went flat from a nail,
and he pulled over to change it, only to find that his brother-in-law
never had returned the jack to its spot behind the front seat. So Cande
plucked a shovel from his truck bed, and spent four hours digging
a hole deep enough that he could remove the flat and bolt the spare
onto the wheel. Sometime during the afternoon, as he pried rocks and
wiped his brow, he released a long mellow stream of blasphemy, and
life went back into perspective.

❋   ❋   ❋   ❋   ❋

One morning the following summer, Estela punches out at six a.m.
and drives home, feet so numb from a shift on the corn line she barely
feels the accelerator, the brake. Twelve hours of rubber apron and
hairnet and steam. And rules! *Delicadísimos, los carajos.* You merely
lift an eyebrow at your *comadre* across the conveyor belt, and Erleen
la supervisora is plucking at your sleeve, all faded blue eyes and sour
breath. Over the squeak and hiss and growl you can read her lips.
She has tried so hard with you girls! "No hablar muchachas. Por favor
no hablar." Her tone is a mix of saying a Hail Mary and shaming
a dog.

Estela opens the curtains and starts a pot of coffee. On TV, a blond
man and woman purr Latin American news straight from Miami.
And there in front of the TV set, swinging her legs from a kitchen
chair, chewing a fistful of sugar-coated cereal, Meche's daughter sits.

Before heading off to the day shift, Meche has left her scrubbed and combed and dressed. Now the kid is waiting for Estela to drive her to kindergarten, the first day of kindergarten. This is the granddaughter whose brothers and sisters call her La Pocha because she was born in Washington State, not Jalisco.

8 Testimonio

Approached on I-82 from the north, on a sunlit day—the freeway climbs out of a gulch—Yakima sparkles into place. You pass milk cows grazing where the river meanders, you dodge a big basalt formation, cross an iron bridge, and there it is, a neighborhood at a time, fairgrounds and train tracks, a Boise Cascade log yard. A small billboard—faded blank and repainted—proclaims Yakima the "Palm Springs of Washington."

The downtown is a study in hard times. Nordstrom's fled five years ago, replaced by establishments featuring discount furniture, paycheck cashing, bail bondsmen. While Starbucks low-profiles in a half-empty mall, new businesses take aim at mexicano clientele—Seguros Chávez, El Mexicano Auto Sound, *salones de belleza, paleterías*. In a tiny grocery store, where people line up for beer and canned hominy and long-distance phone cards, you hear a super-combustible mix of despair and opportunity.

The 2000 Census was perfectly clear. It counted 27,843 total housing units in Yakima: 60 percent had been built before 1960, and 54 percent of the householders had moved in after 1998. Seventeen percent of the population was foreign born. While 28 percent spoke Spanish at home, 33 percent identified itself as Latino, and 29 percent as Mexican. But 68 percent of Yakima identified itself as white.

✳   ✳   ✳   ✳   ✳

Testimonio, Spanish calls it: speech made up of those half-defiant observations that pop out of a person; our slingshot remarks of indignation or common sense; comments we let fly, if not before we know it, certainly before we consider collateral damages. Our words sometimes get the better of us—maybe not all of us but many, many—if only under our breath. Staircase wit is something very different, made up of remarks we think of later. Testimonio occurs when conviction overrides your mouth. Yes, testimonio does share legal overtones with its cognate "testimony." *Testimoniar* means not just to serve as a witness, but also to witness *for* a certain perspective or point of view. Testimonio may praise, or it may denounce, but no one ever mistakes it for reportage. Two features characterize testimonio: (1) it takes the form of storytelling, and (2) it emphasizes the lessons of first-hand experience. Both political and personal, it seeks to convey the reality lived by people who don't control the manufacture of official history.

❊   ❊   ❊   ❊   ❊

The immigration experience produces much of Mexico's compelling testimonio. Among the many collections of interviews with immigrants, *El norte es como el mar* presents an especially vivid example. Interviewed by researcher Jorge Durand, a fellow named Aurelio—despite thirty or forty attempts—never once made it into the United States. He was turned back at the border every time. Aurelio's case is the perfect example—although, Durand points out, a negative one—of how migrating north is a rite of passage for men from western Mexico, an initiation to manhood. Failing to cross the border leaves a guy ashamed, with only the option of trying harder.

"I had pure bad luck," Aurelio begins, "no matter how many times I tried. I wanted to work up north like my father, my brother. Even my friends from the sugar mill went off as braceros.

"Ever since I was little, I worked in whatever I could, earning a peso and a half, two, maybe three pesos a day. First I worked for a farmer selling tomatoes, carrots and such, until, young and restless, I went off herding goats. I started at seven in the morning, and got off at seven or eight at night, seven days a week. My father was a factory worker, after all. There were a lot of us to support. I started working very, very young, with no chance of getting ahead. Because I had no education, I worked in the local sugar mill in the morning, and in the afternoon on construction sites.

"I first went north with three friends from the mill, as soon as the harvest was over, in 1979. A relative who lived in Mexicali found a *coyote* for us, and put us up while we waited. Finally, something like fifteen of us tried to cross, people from Michoacán, Zacatecas, Guanajuato. About ten at night, so the migra wouldn't see us, we crossed through a wide canal, maybe twenty meters across, on tractor-tire inner tubes. Then we set out walking. From Mexicali to Calexico, for six long hours, we dodged spotlights and patrols. By seven that morning, however, we were in the Calexico jail, and the migra was filling out forms—where we were from, our names. The bus they sent us back to Mexico on took two or three hours to fill up.

"We went back to my relative's place. We bathed, washed our clothing, and waited for dark. Maybe they catch you once, after all, but you keep on trying. My brothers-in-law in Los Angeles already had told the *coyote* they'd pay for me. I had their addresses and phone numbers.

"We were almost to Calexico, this time, when a gringo rancher, out preparing to plant, started up his engine right beside the bushes we were waiting in. We thought the pickup had come, and came out of hiding, and there we were! That rancher reported us. We started running, but had to stop when they fired a couple of shots in the air. And so they sent us back again. After eleven different times, one of my friends had enough, and went back home to Ameca. I kept trying."

❊   ❊   ❊   ❊   ❊

Davis High School sits at the top of Yakima's Walnut Street. In a wide, bright room, thumbtacked on cork boards, posters and slogans surround eight rows of desks. Dust and a thicket of handwriting cover the blackboard. Bookshelves: Spanish and English copies of Eduardo Galeano, Tomás Rivera. Dictionaries of both languages. Teenagers file in wearing jeans and running shoes and baseball caps. They carry nylon jackets and book bags. Forty percent of the three thousand students here are mexicanos, says instructor Jim Bodeen. Every year, in this room, twenty-five different youngsters study Latino literature. This year, half the students are Mexicans, newly arrived in the United States, and half are streetwise Chicanos.

For nine months a year, Bodeen listens, from his vantage point, to what is in essence mexicano immigration talking to itself. Over the last ten years, he's edited and published two anthologies of student testimonio, writing assignments that take the form of parent interviews and letter poems, of stories and collaborations. This week's assignment—responding to a Juan Rulfo short story—produces journal entries: passionate and jumpy; both impersonal and intimate; full of hesitations and false starts, setbacks and compromises. The writing contracts, and identities overlap: boldface assertions about the nature of life, marginal afterthoughts, abject retractions.

A lot of it, not surprisingly, sets out to show the writer entertaining what he or she thinks are literary feelings. Or sophisticated analyses of society. Or wide acquaintance with danger, depravity. And yet, overall, the students' observations trace a slippery path from Mexico's Central Plateau to the Yakima Valley, from Spanish to English. Imagine a neighborhood so ornery that cabdrivers wouldn't enter it, so poor that housewives lined up with buckets at a neighborhood water spigot. All that's left of that neighborhood are nicknames: El Perrus, El Zurdo, El Bronco, El Condorito and El Borrego, El Loco and La Vaca and El Mando.

❖   ❖   ❖   ❖   ❖

Maybe they call it something else, but Anglos recognize testimonio as a form of expression. On June 5, 1995, after a week-long series of articles on Michoacán, Mexico, the *Yakima Herald-Republic* invited readers to call its Infoline service to respond. Of the fifty the paper printed, forty-two responses expressed some kind of resentment, typical being that of a reader who wrote that he was " . . . tired of having this Hispanic s__t shoved down our throats."

Some responses recalled the Valley's turn-of-the-last-century immigrants, people with origins Scandinavian, Dutch, French Canadian. "Other nationalities have come in many numbers," one reader wrote, "but certainly didn't get that kind of coverage and space." Another, "tired of hearing Spanish and Mexican spoken everywhere" added that "when my maternal grandparents came here from Finland, no special favors were given to them. They learned the language of the land and became citizens and did not expect the government to give them food stamps, free medical or welfare." "When you come illegally into this country," a third agreed, "you are breaking the law. As second-generation American-born I resent it. My grandparents had to come in legally and so did everyone else. Nobody gave them a darn thing."

❊   ❊   ❊   ❊   ❊

Many Anglo readers sound threatened, and no wonder. They sense what is the greatest change felt in many decades in these "underpopulated" and "out-of-the-way" corners of the western United States. In farm towns and company towns, tourist traps, county seats, housing projects and bedroom communities, a mexicano presence has hunkered down for the long haul. And just what is it that draws them here? What has attracted several hundred thousand over the last twenty years, into the lawn-mowing and fast-food–serving and tree-planting and toilet-scrubbing and bale-bucking end of today's American Dream? Opportunity, of course.

Or what they see as opportunity. Because no matter what work they wind up performing, each immigrant arrives with a certain fantasy-*patrón* in mind, a fellow created by overlapping and largely invented reports. Seventy-five, with a round pink face and white hair, pointy nose and wide shoulders, everybody's dream-patrón sits under an apple tree, attending some mexicano kid's birthday party. Fingers thick from years of yanking ladders into place, he dabs at a bowl of *birria*. Then he shakes hands all around and leaves—walking with belly forward, like a man accustomed to leading others—followed by two chinless sons, each a foreman on his ranch, followed in turn by identical wives in Bermuda shorts and gymnasium butts and legs so white you can see the long blue veins.

Planning to work for a man exactly like that, thousands of mexicano every year head north. Exactly how many? Nobody knows. But they leave traces everywhere. On the Tohono O'Odham Reservation—Arizona desert crossing point for many—officials estimate the following: each undocumented immigrant leaves behind more than eight pounds of litter. With what are apparently 1,500 illegals crossing tribal lands every twenty-four hours, thirteen thousand pounds of trash accumulate each day, almost five million pounds a year.

      ❋   ❋   ❋   ❋   ❋

More familiar grievances filled other letters to the Yakima newspaper. Because "Mexicans come up here to live on our welfare systems," they are "bleeding the state dry financially," one observed, while the coverage reminded another "of rewarding these teenage girls for having babies illegally and us taking care of them."

Still other responses expressed mixed feelings. "I thought your articles on Mexico are [sic] really super," a reader wrote, closing his letter with the news that, on the previous Sunday, "as we came home from church we had a Mexican boy breaking into our house. He was quicker than we were. We couldn't catch him." A third category of reader simply didn't want to be bothered. "I was at club last night at Mrs. Smith's," one wrote, "and I mentioned that I was getting tired of these articles and out of the fourteen women there, six said they didn't even look at it and didn't know if it was good and the rest of them thought it had no business taking room in the *Herald*."

      ❋   ❋   ❋   ❋   ❋

Most vividly of all, Aurelio recalls the near misses. "One time, crossing, we heard an airplane and ran like hell to hide. But they got the drop on us. They said over a loudspeaker that they had seen us, to quit hiding, not to run. When they got there, my feet were so swollen that an officer carried me back in his arms. I could've limped along, but that's what he did. Maybe they were being kind.

"In jail, I met a fellow from a village near Ameca. When they asked who he was, he gave a false name, called himself Antonio Solano. But then, when they called our names to take us out of jail, he forgot what he had said. By the time he remembered, the cops already had punched him around for lying. He went limp, and they hit him a lot. Every time I myself got jailed, I showed them my Military Service card, and they treated me with respect. I guess because of my honesty.

"Another time, one of the guys with us had just had surgery, and walked real slow. We were caught because we waited so he wouldn't get lost. Crossing the highway, he fell down and yelped from the pain, just as a migra patrol car was passing. It didn't have the flashers on. But when that poor son of a bitch cried out, they heard him, and nabbed us one more time. After maybe fifteen more attempts, I had just enough money for a ticket back to Guadalajara. I'll come back in a couple of years, I said to myself."

❊   ❊   ❊   ❊   ❊

Individual differences cut deep. But student testimonio does involve a limited cast of characters. First, there's a kind of generic mother, patient, long-suffering, an impersonal source of forgiveness. She rarely appears in specific scenes. Instead she permeates, intermediates. Representing the outer edge of human forgiveness, she almost never forbids. She does a lot of enabling, rescuing those who've done wrong, saving them from themselves.

The students' version of *amá* seems to erase individual traits. It feels stifling. Only mothers who violate the stereotype, who behave in nongeneric ways, register in these pages as individuals. Take the one who goes every afternoon to the park to meet a certain gentleman, sitting at a picnic table talking to her mysterious man, while her children play on the swings—as she told them to—and simmer.

.   ❊   ❊   ❊   ❊   ❊

Surrounded by families who seem not to talk, the youngsters often feel guilty. They squirm under a harsh, judgmental overview, and accuse themselves of pride. One burns her mother's skillet while trying to make cookies, and hides under the bed. When her mother returns, and asks where she is, the daughter calls out that she's not here, that she went to the store. "At times I hear my conscience," writes another. "Why do you have to be so proud?" my conscience asks. "You'll try to talk to somebody? That's what you always say! Keep on like this," my conscience says, "you'll never get anywhere."

A girl describes a young man who can't say what he wants, who buys a car but has no driver's license. He quit school to work in a fast-food restaurant, but now decides he wants to go back to school. He won't explain how come he bought his mother a cubic zirconium ring. Indecision generates evasion. In paragraphs that wriggle—from accusations of having been deceived to begging for another chance— another friendship fizzles out for reasons too painful to mention.

❖   ❖   ❖   ❖   ❖

Student testimonio of course includes a father, a fellow who manages somehow both to occupy the foreground and to feel very distant. Stern, he works hard. It is his money that buys food and shelter, clothing and schoolbooks. Harsh, demanding, he lives to control his children's lives. He sends them to their room to play. Won't let them visit friends. Even orders a daughter to receive her plaque for good grades in the mail, rather than let her attend the awards ceremony.

Nobody talks to the father. He sits without tears with a can of beer in his car in the driveway the day his brother gets shot. Without tears, he watches his daughter graduate. A daughter writes that she hates herself for hating her father while he lives, because she knows she'll enshrine him after he's dead. Daughters dab their eyes and gulp, and ache for a wink of approval, a nod of tenderness. Meanwhile, their brothers practice holding their own faces expressionless, their voices serene.

The father's opinions, when he talks, take the form of proverbs, adages that drip with a tone they never could acquire in English, impassive, oracular, cryptic. The father *is* inherited opinion, a public faucet that generations of advice spill out of. A daughter wants to go to a friend's slumber party: "tell me who you hang out with," says her father, "and I'll tell you who you are."

❀   ❀   ❀   ❀   ❀

As to their own feelings, most of the youngsters write about love. A girl describes a crucifix broken on her bedroom floor, right where she threw it after finding her boyfriend in her best friend's arms. She asked so many times to let her find real love, and look at her now, heartbroken. Then the crucifix seems to speak, to tell her that God loves her more than ever now, angry and defenseless as she is.

"It's been a year," a young fellow writes of another girl, "but every time I see her go by, my heart beats faster—when am I gonna learn not to love this way?" Another anticipates losing love even before it's lost: I watch your lips move so you won't change the subject, those lips I never want to hear separating us. Friendships, like love, end with somebody left behind: *en aquel bonito barrio de la ciudad de México*, one writer recalls. Friendship vanished when it turned, in another case—for one of the friends, but only for one—into love.

❀   ❀   ❀   ❀   ❀

When I met Jim Bodeen, thirty-five years ago next month, he was recently back from a tour in Vietnam, and pursuing a degree in English. It was June 1970, and he was in a class reading the *Iliad*. I remember less what he said about it than I do his tone, an urgent, low-gear note in his voice, a respect for heat and dust and noise three thousand years old. I later saw other Vietnam vets react to the poem in similar ways, but he was the first, and from that moment on I knew I wanted Jim Bodeen as a friend. To my huge good luck, he settled forty miles south of here, teaching at Davis High. For twenty-five years he's been the editor, printer, and publisher of Blue Begonia Press.

His own poems are straightforward, spring-loaded testimonio. "I told the army this, before / they took my name and gave me a uniform," "Another War Story" begins. "Most of what I knew I knew early. I knew / I wouldn't pull their trigger. I knew / my country was the state of South Dakota." "Canyonlands and All Souls Day" observes Yakima mexicanos celebrating Halloween, and recalls the Mexican counterpart, El Dia de los Muertos, where "the dead eat first, after fireworks / clear the debris in the cosmos. The living / eat the extravagant leftovers while learning / to say thanks, and mean it." If Bodeen's poetics of testimonio makes him sound like an Old Testament prophet, he certainly is one with a deadpan sense of humor, as when "the word inside my voice / became too strong. I could hardly breathe." But, in the curious double sense the word has in English, *witnessing* is what Bodeen writes about. As the former combat medic in "Another War Story" recalls to his children, " . . . we worked / to heal anyone hurt. And we were good. . . . We never shut down, ever."

The sly, staccato, heart-felt range of feeling in Bodeen's writing is unique. He doesn't sound like anybody else, which in part accounts for the variety of notes we hear in his students' writing. Call it the artery-jerk of testimonio. Somebody bears a child a year for eleven years, eating one meal a day, barefoot and dodging mudslides. Exit a world of selling cheese and washing clothes in the river; enter a stepfather handy with hair clippers and leather belt. Then there was Great-grandmother—with Chiclets from Talpa, and real shoes, not huaraches—who advised a granddaughter to jilt an abusive boyfriend, and wound up stabbed five times in the heart at her own front door. The Revolution? Someone recalls riding as a kid in a wagon past a ravine of dead bodies. There's no triumph to any of this, nor for that matter any despair. People hear it as life finding its way into words, and shrug. A strong indicator of mexicano, but not a sine qua non in the long run. Because an inclination to it runs so deep in Mexican culture, testimonio practically is a marker for being, as people say, *de la raza*. Though neither such an inclination nor even the habit of speaking Spanish really proves who you are, behavior being suggestive not definitive, a symptom not a sine qua non. After all doña Chole, living on Guerrero's Costa Chica—bear in mind that she speaks no Spanish, and turns into an owl when she wants—is neither more nor less raza than Lupita, her granddaughter, born in Yakima, who studies Special Ed. and who also speaks no Spanish.

❈   ❈   ❈   ❈   ❈

"I went home at night so neighbors wouldn't see me and know I hadn't made it," Aurelio ends his testimonio. It was his last attempt to cross. "I figure el norte just wasn't for me. I wish I'd never gone. Every time I hear about that country, I recall the ocean. I never did like to swim in it. I won't even eat there. . . . When you go north without documents, you go like rubbish the ocean throws up on the beach. That was how I felt—like odds and ends the sea rejects. Before I went up there, I used to think the ocean was beautiful. Now I can't even bear to walk on the sand!"

III   Adaptations

9 The Portable and the Porous

Much against my better judgment, José and I were driving 1,500 miles south to San Diego. He wanted to attend one of those multicultural shindigs put on to benefit half-hearted academics like the two of us.

The truth was, José had snaked me into coming along. The day the conference announcement arrived, three months before, he started in. Appealing to something deeper than friendship or collegiality, he went right for the throat. He trained a remorseful look on me. "Maestro," he purred, "pues maestro. No hay mexicano que mee solo." He had me there and we both knew it. "No Mexican so much as pees alone," the saying goes. I knew right then that I might as well start packing.

That was why this morning, with half a hangover each, we had awakened in a Redding motel. The sun came up on a blue jay, on a ponderosa branch. As we pulled out, a tar smell built up in the parking lot.

Half an hour on the road, and José looked over his shoulder. He squinted his one good eye.

"¿Maestro?"

Like a lot of people our age, he preferred the way that half-ironic, elbow-in-the-ribs title leveled a range of occupations, from carpenter to orchestra conductor.

"¿Síííííí?"

I couldn't quit yawning.

"¿A poco no viste aquellos Golden Urges?"

José puckered his lips and pointed, Sonora-fashion. A freeway-

ramp McDonald's disappeared in the rearview mirror, and he let fly
with an operatic shrug.

"¡Tengo haaaaambre, Maestro!" He was hungry.

"Maestro, no tengo ni un solo frijol bailando en veinte metros de
tripas." José was untranslatably hungry.

I took the next exit, and ten minutes later we sat on playground
swings at the edge of some little town *desayunando* Egg McMuffin.
We could see a long way. Tucked away in volcanic valleys, vineyard
rows emphasized every dip in the land.

"¡Orale!" José snapped his fingers, grinned, and headed for the
tailgate, six feet tall with black eyebrows and white hair. Blind in
one eye, with wide shoulders and thick forearms, he walked with a
border-state stroll.

Historically, a certain brusque, independent streak in the Mexican
North made for what the U.S. West wound up calling *cowboys*. Isolated, surviving an Indian world, willing to face great danger to get
the legendary riches they were sure existed, Mexican *norteños* always
did live like nobody else. They practiced a horsemanship as eye-
catching as the fiestas and rodeos they organized to display it. And he
was *norteño pero norteño, el buen José*.

The freeway hummed a quarter mile away. Sunlight pressed on my
shoulders, I yawned, and José kept yanking the tailgate. The front
end rose and fell, groaning. Wham. The tailgate opened. He plopped
two suitcases on the ground, swept aside three manila folders labeled
Whole Language Learning, and pitched *A Cultural Infusion Handbook* at the jumper cables.

The night before, halfway through a bottle, he had been recall-
ing how his uncle—an Arizona prospector nicknamed Bolas de Oro,
Gold Nuggets—celebrated the Fourth of July norteño style. Bolas
would stand in the street with an old carbine, fire a shot in the air
¡*Viva México*!, then another ¡*Viva Benito Juárez*!, and finally a third
¡*Viva Teodoro Rúsevel*!, the last fellow being the one responsible—
Bolas assured everyone—for the Social Security check that came each
month.

Now José reached way back in the trunk, around a plastic sack that bulged with dirty socks and underwear, and extracted two warm beers.

"¿Te sacrificas?"

"Gracias, Maestro. Muy amable."

The beer tasted fuzzy. Mine went down in three gulps.

José's profile, in middle age, resembled the one in a snapshot of his father's mother, doña Paca, a Mayo Indian bootlegger born outside Obregón. A woman hard as mesquite wood, she had marched north, as a teenager, to what would become, two years later, the new state of Arizona. She picked crops and saved her money and opened a corner market to sell dollar pints of wine on Saturday night to drunks from the reservation.

Sixty years later, age seventy-five, doña Paca occupied a lawn chair on Saturday nights by the cash register in her store in Miami, Arizona. She kept busy twisting the ear of grandson José, "¡saluda cabrón!" Someone, she winked, had to remind him what good manners were. He better say *buenas noches* to people whether they answered in Spanish or in English or Apache.

José adored her company so much doña Paca sometimes mock-complained to the Saturday night loafers out front that she had to watch her grandson. He became so wrapped up in the Revolution—specifically, in her stories about driving don Porfirio from the country—that he could forget to ring up a pig-foot, a pint of Thunderbird.

After we stomped our beer cans, and pitched them back in the trunk, José took two deep breaths and glared at his faded red '75 Ford Fairlane station wagon, a vehicle that, two weeks before, he had bought from Delbert, a scratchy Yakima octogenarian. For $500 cash, José acquired a car that barely made the state line before we figured we better load up extra quarts of oil. Since then, wherever we went, a black haze ate the horizon behind us.

José shook his head. "*Pinche* hillbilly. He swore to me. Said it had seventy thousand original miles *no más*."

"¿Y las demás?" I couldn't resist. "What do you figure ol' Delbert counted all those other miles as?"

Wham. Wham, wham. Now the tailgate wouldn't even close.

At last José slid behind the wheel, found a freeway ramp, and the two of us resumed our semi-serious routine of the night before—proclamations and verdicts released by tequila.

Once again, José allowed as how he and I were *vatos* transplanted, by graduate degrees, into academic careers, right? I shrugged. *Pos' allí muere.* That was how things had to be. "We better get used to that nondescript watershed we live in," he went on—used to living, he meant, a few miles below the Canadian border—because by now it was obvious he and I were gonna spend our lives at each others' kitchen tables, laughing in Spanish about terms like *hierarchy* and *construct, colonialism* and *alienation.* "¡Fíjate!" he suddenly nodded at the morning horizon. We passed the school district where, thirty years before, he had started teaching school. "Allí mero vivía," he sighed. Right over there had lived a grower's daughter who loved him madly.

"Con todo por acá," he sighed again, "puras añoranzas." He aimed his lips at grape trellises striding like long legs. "A la vueltita nomás." Right around the corner was where she lived.

"¡*Ay qué época*! Me and Pepe Villarino, *imagínate*, we played at a couple of wedding receptions here. They told us to bring our guitars to a party in some apartment building afterward. But I got lost, and here it was 2 a.m. First door I knocked on, this bathrobe blonde opened up. 'Well,' I said, *'es de, es de*, I was hunting a party.' She got a truly unusual look on her face. She yanked the sash on her robe, and growled, 'You just found one.'

"Let me tell you, maestro, she seized the very tip of my belt and led me in the door. Turned out she lived there all alone. She poured me a shot of Hornitos, and we wound up in the shower. Try to imagine it, maestro. She produced a bar of soap and had her way with your humble servant."

"Soap?"

"Wanted to marry me for months."

"Did you say soap?"

"She was a highly inventive young person."

Inventive? Hmmm, I figured he oughta know. José himself was a kind of invention. Guitar across his lap, with an eerie talent for mimicry, and a snifter of Viejo Vergel before him, he held court at kitchen tables. He fingered his way back and forth through tones like a pianist. In either of two languages, he left your walls spinning with shifts of diction, leaps of attitude, stony indifference or wet-leg allegiance. Serene scorn. Bandstand oratory.

❊   ❊   ❊   ❊   ❊

Understand one thing. All this happened years ago. Plus, I was the kind of guy—in those days anyhow—who went around forever planning how to write about stuff. What stuff? Because I never knew beforehand, I called myself an essayist. Good thing I had a state job.

Specifically, I was paid for nudging lower-middle-class youngsters into sympathy with the likes of Emily Dickinson and Akhilleus. For a certain number of hours each week, for twenty-five years, in an isolated Pacific Northwest college town, in a valley full of Norwegian and Danish last names, I had earned a lower-middle-class living. For nine months a year, it was a life of books and a few friends.

But everything changed when José arrived. A *paisa* from the very same bilingual meander of English and Spanish, he felt more at home talking about the world in Spanish, even if he did speak English—and he had to speak it every day—with a flat Western drawl.

Given where we both had wound up working, the feature that knit us together was one the colleagues called *bilingualism*. All over the U.S. Southwest, not to mention the Mexican North, millions of people dwelt on both sides of the language line. "Les educaron en español, y les enseñaron en inglés." Reared in Spanish but educated in English was the idea.

By the time we finally pulled into San Diego, still *cotorreando*, making like parrots, I felt cornered all over again: my earlier qualms, my itchy apprehensions about attending. We tugged our suitcases out of the trunk and crossed a parking lot. I pocketed a room key José slid down the counter, and studied name tags set out for conference participants: Early Childhood and Elementary, Curriculum and Supervision, Social Studies and Foundations. The one with my name on it said Creative Writing.

And so, with my trade pinned to my shirt, I followed José to our room. And now, the fundamental difference in what we each anticipated: he saw it as an expense-paid vacation in Tijuana; I expected ten days among a bunch of academic stiffs, and already felt like backing out. "A ver si no podías ir solito," I began. Maybe José wouldn't mind attending the grand opening alone.

His answer was to open the door and—with bulletproof aplomb— remind me about the urinal habits of the Mexican male. A moment later we were wheeling through traffic, over a bridge, and then more traffic out to the dean's beach-cliff digs: redwood cantilevered out, out, out—I swear you could hear waves and seagulls—out to where a lone mariachi trilled, and the margaritas flowed.

On sofa and love seat, hearth ledge and piano bench, sat thirty faculty members from institutions of higher education all over the country. I got the last empty chair. While guys on either side of me traded small talk and acronyms, I looked at my watch and counted floor tiles. I told myself to concentrate. I re-counted the floor tiles, crossed and uncrossed my legs. I noticed I was the only one in the *pinche* room not talking to someone else. ¡*Qué gacho*! Where was José?

I picked a path to the balcony, where José was chatting up the dean. A short, square person, balanced on the balls of her feet—weaving and bobbing, hooking, jabbing—the dean nodded at me. She asked José about minority graduation rates at, *where?*, she squinted at our name tags. At intervals she interrupted her own remarks—about grant cycles and funding agencies—to observe that her Brooklyn (Sicilian-American) childhood had made her what she was: wholly aware of what it was to be both female *and* at a cultural disadvantage, thank you.

"Nobody paid attention when I graduated high school. My older brothers followed my dad into construction trades. But me, I said, 'Ma,' I said, 'I gotta wait tables, whatever, I'm goin' to college.'"

So much for first impressions. José and I beat it before the scheduled sing-along: *Volver, Cielito lindo, De colores*. Two love songs and one about Jesus. Jesus.

My second impression of the dean took place the next night, over a patio picnic table between two dormitories. She sat down to apologize for some remark she'd let slip, moments after we left, about how Tijuana attracted nothing but beer-swilling fraternity boys. Now she sat dabbing her eyes with paper napkins. Blurting that she was exhausted and had no friends. Prozac was no help at all. She lived alone in that huge goddam house, and owned $10,000 worth of video games. Finally, she lifted her palms, shrugged, and flipped her Day Runner shut. She stood up, said she was sorry, and walked off, dialing her cell phone.

José was so pissed off he was speaking English. Frankly, I only recall words like *paternalistic* and *officious*, because I was wowed by the knucklehead justice of it all. How a strong and funky person crumbled at the implication she lacked respect for what her funding sources nowadays made her call "Hispanics."

Was her behavior comic? It was a hoot. And yet, how come I felt vaguely embarrassed? Back in our room, I sat and unlaced a shoe. José was already brushing his teeth. "Puessss"—I finally managed to say—"bueno es de, es parte del show."

José shrugged. He said nothing. Presumably because to observe that any behavior as wacky as the dean's was merely *part of the show* did go beyond, way beyond, ordinary mexicano stoicism. All my life I'd heard people say that something outlandish was merely *parte del show*. But I also had to admit that the phrase was cryptic.

José flipped the light switch, and began emitting a string of feathery snores. I flipped my pillow and yawned and thought about that phrase. When I was a kid, it sounded like a mantra for the middle-aged—a five-syllable ad for the long-haul life, a laughable mix of laid-back and serene. But now, in late middle age, I heard another meaning in it. Now it was only a recognition of what seemed better-than-average odds that reality was, at minimum, a production, a show with beginning and middle and end. Dismissing something as parte del show always had been the favorite maneuver of people who, like me, sat fidgeting through their own existence like moviegoers.

❀　　❀　　❀　　❀　　❀

Next morning, during a coffee break, we socialized. Imagine a hall of beige brick, fluorescent light, and vinyl tile floor, young people in sandals and tattoos entering, exiting, pecking each other on one cheek or high-fiving.

Five or six of our colleagues were talking about public schools' inter-ethnic conflict, when José called attention to the droop in one of his own eyelids. With a grin he recalled the time, in second grade, when two Apache kids with a slingshot waited for him after school, and you could see the colleagues' faces relax. This guy wasn't at all what they expected. Not a trace of the guardedness and disdain of identity politics.

"Where I grew up, we celebrated Easter every year," he said, "by cooking a pig on the riverbank. Indians, black folks, Anglos, the whole town turned out. Every year during Lent, the Mexican neighborhoods quit drinking. People stuffed the dollars they saved into a twenty-gallon mayonnaise jar.

"Easter Sunday, we'd put out streamers and bunting, picnic tables and half-gallon jugs of brandy, tequila, kegs of beer, and pitchers of iced tea. Local bands played for free. One mayonnaise jar full of crumpled bills did wonders for what, nowadays, we call a sense of community."

Out the window, a bell in a tower was tolling. I looked around, and the corridor was empty. José by now had an audience of exactly two, a man and woman maybe not transfixed but interested—though also a good ten minutes behind schedule, they pointed out. Participants were due upstairs for a showing of *Birth of a Nation*. José proposed a long lunch in Tijuana instead.

The lunch was tremendous. Our two colleagues, it turned out, were *bien simpáticos*, although by now they're only a pair of memory-blurs I call Marvin and Moira. We wound up in a tiny restaurant under a ceiling fan. When José ordered four Bohemia beers, Marvin and Moira looked around and sat with their backs to the wall.

José thought a moment, then lifted a glass, *salud*. He set out recalling that afternoon, two weeks before, when he bought his station wagon from Delbert. He mimicked the tall, skinny Delbert counting the cash, handing over the keys. Then how Delbert followed us out to the driveway, drawling,

"No offense, but, bigod, you people oughta learn English."

Moira and Marvin stiffened. They got busy peeling the labels off their beer bottles, jaw muscles twitching. They didn't come all this way, you could tell, to hear how outrageous white people could be.

José paused, and took a deep breath. I recognized the calculating, resigned look a trapeze artist turns on empty space.

"So I told Delbert," José plunged on, "I said to him, 'You don't even know the worst, my man.'"

José waved for another round. He bent, re-tied a shoelace, and continued.

"Remember one thing about *us people*, I told him: *we are eeeev-erywhere*. Told him to check out my buddy"—José nodded at me— "account of as soon as we got *him* outa the fields, he whitened up, his eyes turned blue, and then he started talking English."

The colleagues turned to me, eyebrows arched. And yes, I had to admit the story was true. Delbert had told me to say somethin' in English. Then he growled I had a *bigod* decent *start*. Though I did not, of course, speak it perfect.

Anyhow the look that crossed those colleagues' faces was something to see.

❋   ❋   ❋   ❋   ❋

In the long run, it isn't that memory plays tricks. You have to know your way around is all. The scenes that you yourself appear in accumulate, until your head is full of trapdoors, passageways, inexplicable traffic patterns.

No news there, I admit. But even so, every time, I flinch at the shortcut my own thinking takes. I go straight from that afternoon in Tijuana—auto exhaust, urinal-cake odor, itchy close-ups—to a corresponding moment a month or so later, the first Monday of classes that fall, in fact. I was filling out a grade book. The phone rang, and a secretary's voice shook with the news that José was dead.

"Of an aneurysm." Her voice clenched. She said he bled to death in an ambulance, racing through sagebrush toward a hospital forty miles away. I hung up. And shock took over.

I watched my fingers probe the phone numbers of Lupe, Omar, El Che, and heard their voices rip. My body swallowed dinner and curled in bed—all this goddam distance. Maybe it would be gone by the time I woke and laced up a pair of running shoes and went weaving down gravel roads past a silage odor.

But of course it wasn't. Any familiar object I looked at—fountain pen, refrigerator door handle—appeared italicized, bracketed, set apart. How could the horizon look the same? Heels drumming the road shoulder, I started planning how to write about José. Dodging pesticide-crumpled sparrows, I started with what I had, a hunch that his story had to do with being *bilingual.*

Later, toweled off and hair slicked back, I picked up my car keys, and the hunch had accumulated words. What the U.S.–Mexican border separated wasn't really two countries, but rather two ways of thinking about the border they shared, two entirely separate versions of it. Monolingual thought considered the border something cross-able, almost at will—a leak, a wound, a valve. While bilingual thought knew the border was only a ripple of attitude and accent preceding you, any direction you headed. They had lots in common, of course—two different versions of one imaginary line, and made for a kind of crude balance. For everyone who felt overrun, invaded, somebody else felt out of place and conspicuous.

I myself certainly felt conspicuous—easing into a parking lot, up a sidewalk. I grabbed a thick brass doorknob. José looked impassive. They had him stashed in a back room with a single chair and a box of Kleenex, hair fluffed out on a satin pillow, quilt tucked under his chin. I must've stood there half an hour. What did it feel like to bleed to death among strangers?

Later, I would recognize what José's friendship had given me—an appetite for patience, for navigating the portable border formed by what you ignore and what you risk—but at that moment, all that went through my mind was one of doña Paca's tales, one about don Porfirio. About how one night he called his generals together. Gouty, arthritic, they lined up and advised him to flee the country, but don Porfirio stalled. Even while mobs pelted the palace windows with oranges, don Porfirio played for time. Sure, he knew a ship was waiting to take him to Paris. But he liked to make them wait, all those college-educated underlings who reminded him he was only a cynical *indio* from Oaxaca.

Back and forth, like a scruffy sentry, I paced. A janitor sneezed, "*hwhnnnh!*" into his handkerchief, and I jumped. The poor guy already had locked up, mopped, and smoked two cigarettes. Now he stood at the door, hands folded, but I couldn't leave. I couldn't quit projecting a bunch of feelings from don Porfirio onto José—the same grief at leaving, balanced by longing to be gone—until I was feeling exactly that way myself.

At a backyard wake, that evening, I took notes until my hand cramped. I counted a couple of hundred people sipping brandy and tequila, picnic tables heaped with enchiladas, *chilaquiles*. By midnight I was scribbling in the dark.

Andy González's tejano accordion kept playing *De colores*, although tonight it was no Jesus routine, only a wheezy hymn from 1920s Jalisco and Michoacán, theme song of a bloodletting that left a quarter of a million Mexicans dead. Four or five of us scrunched up on lawn chairs in the dark, humming the same notes that Cristeros used to sing before firing squads. Dew collected on tinfoil. Somebody hollered, "¡Viva José!"

10 Portraits from the Inland Empire

El amor de los pobres es como el espinazo de
los puercos, pelado pero muy sabroso.

Mexican proverb

ARTURO

It was episodes of Kojak that had given Arturo his first (dubbed) glimpse of the country he sat in now, wearing orange overalls, talking through plate glass, running his fingers through thick hair that his wife scissored monthly on the front stoop. Fingers thick with flat nails and knuckles big as walnuts. The feed-sack bulk of him emitted a voice as thin as flute notes. Arturo was talking about love: how what you knew about love depended on when you learned it. How by the time Arturo was eight, the man he knew as his father would drop in on the family at odd hours for a bowl of soup, and a couple of gruff remarks to the kids lined up watchful on the couch. Only to lead his mother by the arm to a back bedroom, and her thumbtacking a shower curtain over the doorway.

By the time his father taught him rhymed sayings about women's private parts, Arturo was staining his school trousers with oil, skinning his knuckles on lug nuts to keep his father's pickup on the road. Whatever it took to exit a 1970s Guadalajara neighborhood of peso devaluations, Arturo had it. The corner grocery store wore a bullet hole over the beer cooler—from the day a reform politician was shot and slung in the trunk of a stolen taxi. From a rear-apartment window there sometimes floated the cries of a neighbor lady who entertained her husband's boss in mesh stockings. Fruit rinds puckered in the gutter.

Now Arturo got to the point. With hair slicked into submission, lips and jaw blunt as a face sawed into ironwood, he reviewed the events that had left him in jail: (1) not one single ironed work shirt in his drawer last Friday morning, and (2) a lay-off notice clipped to his paycheck that afternoon. So at a certain note in the wife's voice, when he brought up the topic of ironing, as he parked at a 7-11 for a six-pack, he hit her. One open-hand slap was all. He closed the car door then stepped away. But as the glass door before him whooshed, he frowned, pivoted, snatched the passenger door open, and kicked her in the thigh hard. For two or three minutes, his pointed-toe boot kept flicking like a snake tongue at where she rolled on the car seat. It followed her to the floor.

Nothing compared to it, to the time-drift that hit him on Friday nights. Anything could happen. He wound up where his knuckles led him. He gulped beer, he dozed on a couch with cigarette burns in it, *¿y qué?* No worse than *mil cabrones* every Friday night. Especially after who knew what looks and tones of voice all week—from foreman, from mayordomo, from supermarket checkout Chicanas who spoke to a person as *tu*. Anyhow he hit her, the wordless creature by whom he had five children, the *pobre nalgona* he met and fumbled one night behind a filling station. Sixteen years after she cooked a hot meal and moved in, what ruled him wasn't love but modesty. He lived trapped at some edge in her, some knowing look. Even shuddering in his arms, at 2 a.m., she answered their kid's cry a room away in a perfectly even voice. Her detachment left him like some country boy openmouthed at a card trick. He felt his voice flee to the far end of its range, and his neck became rigid. He knew he had to learn something else about love.

NIEVES

Patrolling St. Vincent, Salvation Army, Nieves rescued dark blazers and plaid skirts. With a 1950s Goodwill sewing machine, tucking and pleating, she dodged the look associated with *la mexicana*, the T-shirt and sweatpants, the ponytail and *tenis*. She invested in $20 haircuts. During lunch break, while others chewed and chatted, she recopied her night school journal-writing assignments. Paragraphs about the fast-food chain where she chopped lettuce between two broad-shouldered women, both named Heidi, both former barrel-racing champions newly married, glowing with new surnames: Crudup and Thigpen. But Nieves's journal made it clear that she herself was a casualty of love. A 45-year-old mexicanita, single mother rearing two teenage sons from a mexicano husband long gone. Plus a five-year-old conceived with a neighbor, a lonely Anglo rancher long divorced, blue-eyed, square-jawed, scared. The rancher's pride ached that she and he had found their way into each other's arms only a couple of times. The night he phoned drunk to accuse her of having got herself pregnant in order to get at his money, she hung up. And they never were intimate again.

"¡Ay qué Nieves!" people always said, how she was headstrong as her father, don Pablo the shopkeeper. So old and deaf that neighborhood kids called him don Pueblo, he sat on an empty crate, brown and tough and supple as a belt, unfiltered Delicado dangling from thin lips. The minute your foot crossed his door frame, don Pueblo knew what your mother sent you for.

Neighbors recalled how Nieves's mother went into labor on the maid's day off. Don Pablo came home to a sink of dirty dishes, and took off his hat and slipped on an apron, and stood there thinking. Half an hour later a niece found him bent over the sink scrubbing, suds shoulder high, an ancient single-action .45 in a holster strapped around the apron.

Nieves's mother, though, was very different. If each human soul took its shape from the two love-throes that propelled it into the world, Nieves reflected, her father's straightforwardness was what survived in her. Hours after releasing her into this life, Nieves's mother had hemorrhaged and died, leaving Nieves to grow up with a mother that she imagined, a creature of hints and indirections. Her mother was a composite, one that Nieves had pieced together from the different observations of aunts, allusions that drifted around the big, cone-shaped *tamal* steamer that sat every Christmas in the kitchen on a pan of boiling water.

Nieves's earliest images of her mother came into focus while she inhaled the odor of masa and corn shucks—the very scent that home-sick guys, nowadays, stranded just below the Canadian border, paid ten dollars a dozen to get a whiff of on December 25. Nieves sensed even today, deep in her own feelings where a mother's foto should have sat, a thousand-year-old recipe of pumpkin seed and turkey, a fragrance peremptory and subtle, tenacious as the roast-pork flavor singed into Mexican lard by high-rendering heat, the thick and faintly sour cream slathered on lunch-cart sandwiches. She decided that her mother persisted like a family cowlick or flat feet.

Maybe her mother's qualities predominated in Nieves's older brother. Two hours down the freeway from where Nieves lived, he had a job forklifting nuclear waste at Hanford. Married to a tejana who cooked with Velveeta and slept under a crucifix and waited for him every night (he grinned) all smells and lunges and heavenly cries. Anyhow, Nieves was sure that her brother no longer felt out of place in the United States. His indirections smoothed over a certain contrast between himself and the Anglos around him. Which in turn let him think he belonged in the United States. But Nieves herself didn't know if she wanted to change her feelings like that. Being conspicuous in public here was difficult enough. Imagine feeling like you were a *part* of some reality organized without you. In hillbilly sagebrush towns, her eyes flicked Safeway aisles for a brown face.

Isolated? She had to drive thirty miles each Sunday for a newspaper in Spanish, and *pan dulce*. She even had to drive through "The Town Where the West Still Lived." Its thirty-five murals painted over the last six years on the walls of Les Schwab Tires and Providence Hospital, Top Cleaners and Powow Emporium and the Roadrunner Building—each mural a western motif. Rodeo and stagecoach race, potato harvest and haying and roundup, Saturday market and black-smith shop. A doctor visited the ill, around the corner from where a governor signed a treaty with Indians, itself around the corner from the Palace Hotel and Lillie Mansion. The freeway out of town passed through fields cleared by the efforts depicted in a mural entitled *Clearing the Land*. The local Mural Society imagined a past wrenched free of nuance.

Apparently it didn't include mexicanos, not a single mural, not after half a century of mexicano presence. On one Sunday, the nearest mexicano images were alive, and one town downriver. Where two elderly men at a sidewalk table in front of the bakery that Nieves preferred sipped coffee, each slender, with gray mustache and white, Stetson-like hat and cowboy boots. Soon two more such fellows joined them, one toting a guitar. In a soft, neat voice, one performed a love song in which a fellow mourned at being left for another. The guys at the table nodded gravely, and kept on talking pickup trucks and grandchildren. Stacked timothy bales and grazing Holsteins collected at the horizon. They envied the adventures of one grandson in particular. As late-summer light and shadow wove the valley—they'd lived here for twenty-five years—they savored the kid's tale of snagging a boxcar. To sway over cinders. To jerk a handle and tumble inside and start life over.

LALO

A community college writing instructor for twenty years, Lalo lived comfortably out here in the sagebrush, divorced, his children grown by now. He lived alone in a double-wide on a gravel road under willow trees. Twenty years before, newly arrived in the United States, he'd obtained a job reading those two- and-three-page typewritten disquisitions, which the state obliged the young to learn to write on topics that interested the young not at all. Remedial writing classes, twenty-one years ago in fact, though time certainly hadn't made him comfortable where he worked. He radiated reserve at his colleagues, drab people who talked in passive-voiced verbs. They gravitated toward conference tables to shift their feet like so many rush-hour straphangers eyeing the same headline. Without belligerence or rancor, he trained on them a tone that dressed him in double-breasted suits of linen, a panama hat, two-tone shoes—an illusion based on his years working in central Mexico as what the colleagues would have called a ruling-party hack. Tall and slender with collar-length, straight gray hair and rimless glasses, in sandals and socks, jeans and flower-print shirt, voice clear, opinions well considered—Lalo felt used up. He felt reduced to living other people's lives for them, his own all spinoff by now. Victim of a second-rate middle age. Maybe he hadn't turned out exactly like he wanted, but he was his own by-product, wasn't he?

A trunk of rained-on books that he found in the corner of a barn at age ten had taught Lalo what sentences sounded like. One scholarship followed another. He graduated from the huge UNAM university into various rural party positions, which in turn led to a real administrative spot as soon as the PRI governor-candidate he backed won an election. But Lalo, alas, trained a lot of disdain on the "peasants" that he now had to work with. He resigned, after ten months, the morning he discovered, in his desk drawer, a human turd. He resigned and fled Mexico—just as millions of others had—him and his college degrees.

In fact, at different stages in his life, Lalo had fled both Mexico and marriage. Now, near retirement age, he simply had sworn off women. Lalo was truly beyond getting involved, even if it did make him a sucker for love tales. He missed having a woman around so much that love tales crowded his bookshelves. Framed with expectation, books felt better than any contact with the shrill, demanding, ephemeral creatures he had married. Lalo simply preferred tales about women to the company of women. Ever since one night back in Guadalajara, with a wiry, middle-aged redhead from Los Altos (or so she said). He met her in a hotel lobby. And, recently having left her husband, yes, she could have a drink with him. And by midnight yes she would leave with him, but to his place, please, please. And he woke at home two days later with a blinding headache and not a stick of furniture in the house. *Pinches viejas.*

Lalo taught writing to people who came from what they called *los ranchos,* campers on blocks, trailers with plywood bedrooms nailed on, chiles sprouting in flowerpots, a tarp billowing over car seats. They were people whose reserve created a hooded irony, a people taciturn, manipulative, even miserly and backbiting. And yet, like butterflies, remarkable love tales wiggled free of their gossip. Like that of Nacha, an elderly mexicana cremated—to the scandal of her whole parish—whose ashes were therefore consigned to a tin urn on a closet floor, till a granddaughter took pity and drove her to the Columbia Gorge on a windy day and set her loose. And a real scandal it was, as Grandma Nacha hadn't followed her husband, Grandpa Memo, who died ten years before, uttering a last wish that he be roped into his recliner then driven, in the back of his pickup, back to Michoacán and buried. La Nacha outlived him by ten years, however, watching *telenovelas* all day, so it was a very different Nacha who went off, rosary in hand, to be incinerated, to stay in the United States.

Lalo knew doña Nacha's story because her granddaughter, Adela, wrote about her. Adela, who spent her first week in class with eyes narrowed, shoulder blades pressing the rear wall, and then began to trust him and started writing. Straight nose with eyes far apart, torso slender with enormous breasts, Adela favored tight T-shirts and designer jeans. A B+ biology major, and late everywhere she went, she was a level-headed person who simply happened to have a certain effect on men: she left their innards singing. She sent waves of longing that pinned the same look to face after face. And what effect did having that effect have on Adela? She kept forgetting the effect she had. Her uncles looked at her differently now. And not because she was in a pre-med program. That was what her journal confided one afternoon.

On that particular afternoon, Lalo sat on the cedar deck above his backyard creek. With a spring breeze twisting around him, he was reading student journals. Once again marveling at the Greek chorus effect—which was what he called it when some narrative turn of irony left him, as if in a theater, grateful and awed that human destiny was so devious. Three generations of mexicana willpower surfaced in Adela's journal. In stages huge and barely glimpse-able, from grandmother to granddaughter, the women in Adela's family were making it clear what they wanted. They resembled a person in a snapshot gaining control of the frame by winking at the camera.

A page away, Lalo read about Adela's older sister, Meche, a law school graduate who visited a primary classroom on Role Model Day. Showing the kids her laptop, her BMW—why not convince *los huerquillos* that a mexicana could be an attorney?—Meche forgot how country mexicanos scorned two things above all: (1) tooting one's horn, and (2) fishing for compliments. And yet the problem wasn't that Meche forgot where she came from. Meche had never *been* where she came from, Adela's journal pointed out. Leave it to Meche to emphasize that, winters, she flew to Central America to vacation somewhere so isolated that buzzards circled over the tourists at poolside, and the fishing guides, all black, spoke with a British accent.

ALMA

Alma sat down, unfolded her napkin, and started talking. Years before, confronting a husband's brazen sneakiness, she'd walked out the door with his finger marks on her. Almost overnight, she became herself—a graying schoolteacher, bottle curls and Celtic love-knot earrings, rimless glasses and cell phone. It had taken a few weeks of banging on motel walls at 6 a.m., weeping about a hysterectomy, but her own dry-eyed tenacity had marched her off to college. She earned the teaching certification that put her in charge of a bilingual classroom in a school in what the local newspaper swore was the fastest-growing Hispanic area in all the United States.

But the happy ending to her story had squeezed her empty. For months now, she wanted nothing but Snickers at each meal, until her doctor diagnosed diabetes, which already had blinded her cousin, and left her brother with a kidney transplant. She saw diabetes leave one uncle, a guy she remembered standing over six feet tall, a legless scrap of a man. So what was happening in her life? She winced at what she was becoming—the wistful, meddlesome neighbor smelling of hand cream, the loud aunt who borrowed pantyhose with a wink. For distance, she cultivated the self-deprecation of a movie sidekick. She saw her own future: a routine of fad diets and small bitchy dogs. Her life seemed a monochrome version of her parents' lives in the thirties and forties and fifties. Scenes absorbed with her sisters, drinking cinnamon tea at the kitchen table with *la abuelita*, the grandmother who perched on a kitchen chair, clucking her tongue, a grandmother who trained judgmental eyes on supermarket produce, who filled in years of lost cousins, vanished neighbors. Her glance directed a granddaughter on an errand.

Grandma would hand-roll cigarettes one after another. The girls would chat with Grandma in Spanish. Then—so la abuelita couldn't understand—they'd switch to English to talk about their boyfriends. Until Grandma would pull out a deck of cards, shuffle, then make the sign of the cross over it. Then tell each girl to cut the cards, offering to tell her fortune. And la abuelita was always right! One by one she'd describe exactly the fellow each sister had a crush on at the moment, including traits that the kid had confided only now to her sisters. Which convinced the sisters that Grandma had psychic powers. Though years later, as adults, each began to ask herself how Grandma had managed to shop in downtown stores where no one spoke Spanish. How did she understand afternoon soaps in English? It made the sisters feel weird to think that Grandma understood English. Maybe she even spoke it.

Like cards from la abuelita's deck, men had appeared in Alma's life, their traits exaggerated. From her purse, Alma plucked a faded, billfold-size snapshot of her father, a handsome, hard-drinking share-cropper who died in his pickup outside a saloon one winter night just a month before his fiftieth birthday. Passersby thought he was plain drunk. The diabetic coma that took him only fulfilled his premonition that, like his own father, he'd never see fifty. He took his daughters to chop cotton, calling them his *hombrecitos*. To this day, his daughters faced the world with a self-assertive aplomb they owed to their father. He never tried to control. He sent them to dances chaperoned by his mother, la abuelita, who examined each guy who asked for a dance, refusing the drunk, the unruly. Otherwise the sisters had to dance with whatever fellow asked. Apart from that sort of basic civility, their father insisted that they be assertive. He even defended their wearing miniskirts. He taught them to wink when called *repelona*, shrewish.

And a damn good thing he did. Now Alma had to nag her son day and night. Nineteen, he wavered between decisions—to go to school or to work, to share an apartment or live alone, to marry his pregnant girlfriend or not to. He spoke not a word of Spanish. He seemed both hurt and puzzled the night a traffic cop—pulling over a carload of

youngsters, then noticing her son—referred to him as "the Mexican."
The love of risk that propelled her father seemed missing in her son.
Her own self-reliance made him depend on her even more.

Ironically, her father—her finger wagged for emphasis—was the
problem. She'd married the first available version of her own father. A
good provider and sensible planner, her ex entered the Navy, attending college on the GI plan. But he came to manhood with a definition
of marriage so narrow it cramped her. Even if, fifteen years divorced,
she now closed her eyes and whispered what really *was* the problem
with that marriage? Was it her dad's empowerment that left her feeling belittled, belligerent? Even now an afternoon with her ex made
her arms and legs itch.

Her second husband was Anglo, a geology professor. The guy truly
listened to her. They hiked, weekending in mountain lodges or beach
houses, savoring aimless talk about pedagogical theory or plate tec-
tonics. Until, every time, like massaging a cramped foot, he would
seize her idea of "racism," meaning to convince her that economics
and social class were really the only factors in how police treated
people. Whatever ill will she sensed was an illusion created by class
and economics. And Alma would strike back with the example of a
morning she preceded him into a Utah airport restaurant. She waited
forty-five minutes without getting served, only to see her husband's
entrance summon up coffee orders, and a starched-apron waitress. So
conflict overtook her second marriage: crafty angles and panic but-
tons, offense taken, pride swallowed, throat cleared, grudge nursed.
She felt his friends were people who held all that she was in contempt:
golfing buddies, bridge partners, fellow Elks, the courthouse crowd.
She also knew that her accusations seemed, to him, capricious and
spiteful. She had wound up between two husbands, one unable to
comprehend the person she'd become, another who couldn't imagine
the person she'd always been.

ALMA

Nobody ever said it was easy to keep this border business straight.
But no one was more American than Alma, her people citizens since

the day Texas entered the Union. But it was in a Spanish salty with tejana slang that she lunched with Lalo, her schoolteacher buddy, with whom she shared twenty years, a two-part harmony marred by the usual male-female mismatches. Lalo had his own emphasis, needs, memory. But he saw her as she was.

Where Alma sat with Lalo in El Restorán Siete Mares, one whole wall was a mural rendering scenes from Michoacán, three thousand miles south, where the owners had been born. Overlooking black fields and broad-shouldered campesinos, an orange sun glowed with merry, human features. Thick-legged fishermen waded the blue of Lake Pátzcuaro. Into every open space, vegetation sprouted and curled and crept—a folk-idealized version of rocky soil that four or five generations of mexicanos by now had forsaken to go north.

With Alma and Lalo sat two of Las Comadres, her closest friends, a group of Chicana educators who met every Friday evening after school at Alma's house. They had a couple of drinks. They smoked a few cigarettes. Today, when they talked about Alma's second marriage, everybody laughed, unable to resist the urge to measure her second husband by mexicana standards, however mixed Las Comadres' feelings about those standards were. One *comadre* even recalled with a rueful grin being sent home from a bar by a male cousin who beckoned her from the door. She was over thirty at the time, married with four children, and merely sitting in a booth surrounded by female friends her own age. But her father had seen her, and didn't approve. He'd sent the cousin to fetch her home. And she went.

All the comadres had married young, like Alma. Each had several children before earning a college degree. Each acknowledged the strains placed on a marriage by middle-aged husbands pursuing lines of work unrelated to education. But only Alma had ever been divorced, let alone married to an Anglo. Having arrived at middle age, then settled into careers, Alma and her friends trained a certain distance on themselves, one that gave them an ever-keener taste for the incongruities of life in the nineties in the Inland Empire. Even those lucky in love felt unsatisfied and wry, quizzical, a slave to mixed feelings. Everyone worked hard to stay married.

Tucked away in their booth, Alma and Lalo and Las Comadres sipped *caldo de pollo*, pinching limes into it, chopped cilantro, diced onion, fingertips pungent. The steam that rippled the mural above them opened their nasal passages. Maybe life could be perfected, somebody shrugged. Believing that it could, anyhow, did turn mexicano lives into success stories, fruit picker to entrepreneur, field hand to social worker. After all, no other immigrant group came from so close or kept coming for so long. No wonder the late-twentieth-century United States owed what it was to one hundred years of invasion by mexicanos, a people whose patrimony had been seized to form the late-twentieth-century United States. Sure, from a certain perspective, Las Comadres lived what looked like the American Dream. But viewed up close the dream made demands subtle enough that the dreamer discovered them only after years of devoted pursuit. Alma and Las Comadres confronted the ways in which the person you wanted to be receded as you got near enough to notice surface flaws, blemishes of emphasis, tics of accent and usage. People like Alma eased through complex calibrations. Bilingual and bicultural, they inhabited a reeling, shifty boundary that sliced the Yakima Valley. No wonder they felt split between two lives, two languages, two sides of a border no one quite could locate anymore. After all, when la abuelita slapped cards on the kitchen table, she made it seem that she saw a girl's innermost desires because, in a way, she did. La abuelita put in her days at the very same identity business that frustrated and fascinated her granddaughters.

NIEVES

Every so often, Nieves flew home. Months of homesickness would lead to ten hours on standby. The L.A. airport was full of flower-print dresses and Levi's, shawls and baseball caps, mexicanos nibbling microwaved breakfasts, lurching through turbulence toward the largest city the earth had ever seen. No matter how often the bus stopped, and Nieves got off among the pothole and fruit-rind streets where she grew up, it was never what she expected. Even the year when she found a leather boutique suddenly there, in place of the neighborhood saloon, and tourists speaking French behind the swinging doors that her father had swept aside to flatfoot a pulque, Adam's apple heaving, the night she was born. Even that year, the trip had the same, curious lack of effect on her, not at all nostalgic. No, her visits left her seeing Mexico with eyes wholly foreign, flinching at the stink and cynicism of the place. Garish, flimsy, the whole country felt like a cheap knock-off, one modeled on border-town crowding, hurry, theft. Nobody had any money. Daily, small humiliations took the form of a traffic cop's whistle, or shopkeepers' scales. Only the gossip was as lush as she remembered. Amid rumors of cheating husbands, of children disinherited, she savored the dark glee of mexicano gossip, the satisfaction inherent in naming other people's flaws or misfortunes, in always having at tongue's tip an appropriate aphorism, well-rhymed, illuminating.

Middle age had sharpened her taste for *refranes*—those venerable aphorisms without which Spanish was never truly expressive. They were like recipes for emotional states. Enigmatic and forthright, notes of praise and blame, devotion and scorn, refranes became the capillary system to extremities of her thought. As she walked down a Guanajuato sidewalk, folk proverbs took over her thought to scold her that she was a mexicana in exile, separated from her husband, rearing teenage children on what she earned with toilet brush and vacuum cleaner. Refranes held her life up to her memory, to the voices of elderly aunts and uncles lodged like wrinkled, unforgiving islands in her family's slide toward extinction. Snatching permanence from the offhand, refranes were collective memory, a creature that rose to full voice when it sniffed the odor of love. Collective memory related to standard language as dancing related to music. It was slang, argot, plain cant. While U.S. lovers handled love like a first-time ice-cream cone, collective memory lent a protocol to love in Mexico.

At least that was how Nieves listened to herself—as contrasting scraps of truth. Every time that she returned from a trip to Guanajuato, she felt like her life took place over a caption, each day a new illustration of something old. So she simply quit going to Guanajuato. Her children and friends now lived in the United States anyway. Homesickness only left her mind bouncing off one bit of rearview wisdom after another, adages about women and men, how love outsmarted us every time. From self-willed surrender to her husband, to self-willed surrender to the neighbor, the latter to assure herself that her first disappointment wasn't a fluke? Life reenacted platitudes. No seamless, movielike flow of events, Nieves's love illustrated old sayings. But that was a kind of survival. Refranes were all that people like her brought across a border secured by heat-sensitive, night-vision patrols. *Corazón de mesón*, she wrote in her journal, and grinned. Ol' *hotel-heart*.

LALO

The Greek chorus effect! His appreciation of it, Lalo decided, made him the only appropriate witness to the fate of Nadine, an Angla community organizer. With her liberation theology, her peasant blouse and broken-string huaraches, she conducted what she called her "lay ministry," underplayed by a constant smile, timid, a thousand times rejected but dogged, a smile with nothing to lose. Nadine weighed maybe 250 pounds. Her forearms swam in pale flesh. Her calves shivered as if frightened at each step. Born in Hollywood in the fifties, she'd gone to high school with the likes of Jimmy Stewart's children. Now she spent whole days with *los pollos,* youngsters who arrived in twos and threes, broke, hungry, cautious guys who slept six to a floor and cooked with five different kinds of chili.

With a staff of one full-time worker—plus an ancient van bearing farmworker stickers on every bumper—Nadine worked out of an Episcopal church. She kept scores of raza in jobs, housed, fed. She stopped fistfights, lent an ear to weeping drunks, and mediated cross-cultural love affairs. She blurted a heartfelt, headlong Spanish, pure infinitives swept along in the wake of gestures. And yet, Nadine sensed her Anglo neighbors' resentment. Guilty about Anglo exploitation, they tended to question her motives. They hinted that her lifestyle merely kept her starring in her own small-budget production number, some tacky flick about flaunting authority. She knew they snickered at her huaraches and flowing skirts, her baseball cap with the name of a Mexican state printed in day-glow colors across the front.

It took about a year for her to leave her husband. She fell in love with a short, dark pollo, a fellow who drifted from orchard to orchard, pruning by day and drinking beer by night till he couldn't stand up. He was good-looking, with classic, country-boy mexica- no manners, a voice that never raised with emotion, impassive face, limp handshake. She and her pollo couldn't care less what people thought. They wrapped each other in a net of expectations. Her pollo trailed her everywhere, slim, all Hollywood dimples, eyes glittering with opportunity. Maybe he read her as the loose-living gringa of stereotype, round of heels, deep of pockets. Anyhow his reading of her let him predict her behavior. Maybe not entirely, but well enough to cadge a lunch here, a six-pack there, a one-hundred-dollar salary advance to drop on a dab of cocaine. He entered the relationship with goals simpler than hers, better defined and more modest. He wanted a job and bearable living conditions. She meant to invent a whole new self.

At last Nadine's pollo talked her into driving him south to the border. From there, after he paid to have his wife and children smug- gled into the United States, Nadine drove the whole family north, to live next to her in the trailer she'd lent him the down payment for. The arrangement worked for a couple of months. Until the pollo's wife dozed on the living room couch one night, and woke to discover Nadine and her husband rolling around on the floor.

But just as in Sophocles, Nadine was blindsided by her own pride. When the 'ñoras took the wife's side and expressed their displeasure, and Nadine's status shrank like cheap hamburger, she launched a counteroffensive. No one could prove a thing, she grinned. What business is it of anyone else's if I give him a ride to work each morn- ing? Never understanding that the 'ñoras expected a woman to live in a way that didn't cause folk to gossip, Nadine made it necessary for women whose families she'd housed to call her a whore.

At last, Lalo sat on his deck and admired the tale. The tale was a lesson why Sophocles let the collective mind twitch in the form of a chorus.

ARTURO

At Arturo's violence counseling session one summer night, all the guys
agreed. "Cualquier falta de respeto." Any inattention at all was cause
enough to hit your wife. They were in their 40s and 50s, tall, lanky
fellows in boots and baseball caps, guys from Jalisco and Michoacán,
courtly, countrified. They started the evening slouched in folding
chairs, wondering aloud how a man could be in trouble for hitting
a wife that was *his* after all. But by evening's end they did admit that
yes, they *had* lived here for twenty-five years. And here, on this night,
they sat in a room in a county museum in a state where you couldn't
hit your wife. No longer could they say they were from some unpronounceable bus stop three thousand miles south.

Addresses, though, changed faster than feelings. Everybody knew
that. Bruises flourished like petals in migrant cabins during the dark
winter months. Silence, then tears over a packed suitcase, the same
old story plodded past where Arturo sat, until the Violence Officer—
blonde hair, blue eyes, a deep voice—put a question to the group in
her university Spanish. She radiated good-natured confusion. Did the
guys think bruises meant that a man and woman really loved each
other? A pause. And then one of those classic mexicano shrugs. It was
a beautiful thing, risen out of the ground, a whole roomful of palms
and shoulders and eyebrows lifted in perfect indifference.

Mexicanos were pragmatists about love after all. And yet they
felt, for all their pragmatism, mexicanos always wound up working
for a people even more pragmatic. Maybe it was because Anglos put
all their energy into wringing crops from a dry landscape, but they
always seemed inert, mysterious. Rarely shaking hands, never inquir-
ing after a person's family. With neither greeting nor farewell, Anglos
entered your life and left it, leaving you to guess how they felt.

Once a week now Arturo went to a class where Lalo put him to
writing paragraphs and reading books. But Arturo knew it would
take him the rest of his life to figure out the Anglos. Sitting here in
their museum felt like squinting down a rifle barrel. As linoleum
curled and ceiling fan wiggled, glass case and framed photo made it

clear—Anglos had acquired even the land they farmed in a limp, inexpressive manner. Not by ferocity, but by default. They simply had discovered that wheat would thrive anywhere bunchgrass grew. As trial and error told how deep to plow and when to plant, Anglo time unfolded in three phases. Installed in their Promised Land of basalt basin and rainless summer, pioneers gave up old habits of thought. Planting in fall rather than spring, developing a wheat resistant to drought and wind and smut—adaptation seemed, to them, the ultimate flight of fancy. Out of nowhere, little towns sprouted with names meant to charm investors and settlers, Sunnyside and Fruitvale, Grandview and Richland and Pomona.

Their museum lent a focus to the Anglo population. Second generation from those who irrigated and then planted hop fields and orchards, they gathered from all over the valley. Cigarette-stained fingers brushed back thinning hair, or tugged faded aprons, as people voiced concern. Over kitchen coffee, or under neon beer signs, they hunched their shoulders, and gulped phrases of resignation, absolutely sure that—birth by birth—their moral example was losing its hold on the valley.

After a dozen sessions in the museum, nights when clarity overtook him like glass cases and captions, Arturo finished his counseling. Clarity taught him to knot his fists in his pockets and smile. By the time he quit drinking, and saved a down payment, and moved his family into a nearly new mobile home, the trace of his father left in Arturo had dimmed like a character in a book. Even though Arturo's wife still acted like nothing had happened. Never once alluding to any change in his behavior, she learned to drive instead. Then she got their eighteen-year-old daughter to arrange housekeeping jobs in Anglo neighborhoods. Finally, one day, mother and daughter went off for eight hours, vacuuming, toting garbage sacks, folding laundry. They came back grinning with groceries and acrylic fingernail kits. And that was when Arturo decided that he was in a love story.

11 Patron Saint and Poster Boy

It shouldn't be any surprise that mexicano illegal immigrants worship their patron saint with a pilgrimage. Twice a year, people set off down a Nuevo León highway, one hundred miles below the U.S. border, through nopal and huisache ravines, past turnoffs to El Paredón, Las Corrientes, Los Remotos. Where the pilgrimage ends, in Espinazo, several thousand people gather, deadpan country folk with crusty hands, crow's-feet, muted body language. Each wears a look of card-player concentration.

The faithful gather in Espinazo to call on the spirit of El Niño Fidencio. In black skirt and white blouse, shower thongs and rebozo, in straw hat and polyester slacks stained from kneeling, people hail from Colorado and Michigan, California and Texas, not to mention from parts of Mexico both far and near. Unemployed and on their knees, disabled, troubled, exiled by Mexican diaspora to Dallas, Indianapolis, Chicago, they touch his photograph and rub their hands over their bodies.

Middle-aged women—dresses soaked, hair down, nipples clenched—wade through a pool of murky water, and fill plastic milk jugs. Everybody's waiting. People crowd and squirm. Finally an elderly woman wrapped in a velour robe hisses and trembles, and heads turn. She's a *materia*, somebody whispers, a medium. Voice rising, trancelike, she identifies herself—El Niño Fidencio, *a la orden*. And Niño gets down to business:

What is the only weapon you have to defend those who follow
the faith? Time, time was all you had when I showed up, flat broke
like you, broken in spirit like you—so how come I say time is still
our weapon? Think about it. Every time you set out for El Norte to
feed your family, think about it. Meanwhile, feel at home between
dirt and sky and minimum wage. Because no, the Lord doesn't dwell
in luxury digs, doesn't hang out with people so vain they covet fine
clothes, or fine bodies.

The woman falls silent. Pilgrims stretch and yawn and look around
them. What they see is Espinazo, Nuevo León—the name means
"backbone." It lies exactly where two cordilleras meet—a rancho of
rusted-out car wrecks and dust devils, a land of goats and rosaries,
tinsel altars, tin roofs. Espinazo burrows into an isolation so huge
that anachronisms warp local speech. People say *belduque* for knife,
cedrón for bucket. The isolation hovers, and crushes.

Maybe it is Niño's preference for isolation—and, therefore, pilgrimage—that links him to migrant life. It makes sense: the patron
of a way of life exemplifying how to lead that life. And the principal
ingredient of Niño worship is *el aguante*, persistence, resolve—what
people used to call *grit*, or *sand*. Those who put high value on el
aguante care little for final outcomes, verdicts. Won-lost records, triumph *or* defeat—keeping score leaves them cold. They revere seeing
things through. Niño sponsors stick-to-it-iveness, *ni mas ni menos*.
Endurance is what wows the faithful.

❁   ❁   ❁   ❁   ❁

In police reports they often have no names, and are chiefly described
by the clothes they wore when their bodies were found floating in the
Rio Grande, or in some canal, All-American, Franklin. A man in his
twenties, wearing a beige shirt, brown pants, and one blue tennis shoe.
A female in her twenties or early thirties, wearing a Tasmanian Devil
T-shirt and maroon jeans. A teenage male with a Chicago Bulls T-shirt
and black shorts.

But sometimes a bit of personal history survives, as in the case of a pair of brothers from Naucalpán, near Mexico City, who drowned in the Rio Grande near Brownsville, Texas, trying to get to New Jersey to paint houses. Or the young mother from Colombia dead of heat exhaustion in the desert trying to join a sister who takes care of elderly people in New York City. A typical border-crossing season opened one March 14, when four young men ages nineteen and twenty, from Chiapas in southernmost Mexico, drowned in currents just thirty-five yards from Texas soil. That June, in the desert that covers most of southern Arizona, sixty-seven more would die.

Cruel as they usually are, border crossings dribble little ironies. Sometimes they even wind up sounding like parables about survival. Take the July night a semi pulled up and loaded a group of men into a trailer with little water and no food. As soon as the doors closed, the air became scarce, the heat intense. When the truck successfully passed the checkpoint at Sierra Blanca—but did not stop—the men began banging on the inside of the trailer walls to alert attention.

Finally, desperate, they opened the boxes underfoot in hopes of finding more water or food. Instead, they found medical supplies, plastic tubes, which they jammed through cracks in the trailer to suck in fresh air. They did get rescued, more than twelve hours later— on cue, we admire their perseverance—when passing motorists saw men's belts sticking out of cracks in the trailer.

❊   ❊   ❊   ❊   ❊

If Niño was illegal immigration's patron saint, Jesse had to be its poster boy. Everybody agreed he was a throwback, el buen Jesse, a relic of what people understood too late had been the heyday of mexicano illegal immigration. Something about his attitude—gleeful, funky, dauntless—recalled an era before peso collapse, when young men lit out for el norte, and came back fidgety, using weird words. Because by now, three years into the twenty-first century, illegal entry had become a dreary business. The Border Patrol closed the traditional routes, and now you hired a guide, a *coyote* who charged $2,000 per person.

After 1990 or so, when hard times made wives and children part of the migrant flow, the whole family underwent the same nasty routine. From three thousand miles away, rumors of work in the Yakima Valley drew innumerable cousins, in-laws, *compadres*, complete with spouses, infants, toddlers, preschoolers, you name it. And so, to an over-hassled generation, Jesse represented the Golden Age, a vanished era when illegal immigration felt more like a sport.

He certainly looked the part. With fine features, nimble, about five six, Jesse had a tattooed panther climbing the veins of his left forearm. He weighed one forty, except for times he holed up in a bathroom every hour or so with cigarette lighter and tinfoil, and forgot to eat. He put in years unloading crates of orange juice eight hours a day, clean-shaven, white Nikes, fresh T-shirt. In later years, when he took off his baseball cap, his receding hairline made him look like a baby bird.

In trailer parks up and down the Northwest, Jesse achieved the status of a small, anonymous legend. He drank beer and smoked crank and wooed teenage girls: hummingbird-ferocious, meticulous as a monk, *¿y cómo que escándolo?* Wasn't he only doing what all migrant youngsters wanna do? Everyone thought that everyone else thought so, anyway, ninety-some percent of those responding being young and male. Plus, who could stay mad at Jesse? He had an otherworldly glee that nearly lifted you out of your shoes. Lovers jilted two and three times took him back. Friends owed hundreds always managed to peel off a loan. It was said that a foreman who found him in some motel room on top of his *quinceañera* daughter wound up offering Jesse a raise.

Jesse's luck was legendary. He rolled or t-boned cars, drunk, without collecting a scratch. At dawn once he wound up sideswiping a national monument, and taking a wrong turn into a river. Another night his car left the highway, and he woke in an onion field sneezing. The tales that grew around him made anything sound possible. Like the time a steaming Col. Sanders bag on the roof of his car distracted a sheriff's dope dog from a joint in the glove compartment. People swore he put a VW bug he was driving way up in the boughs of an orange tree—didn't negotiate a steep-banked curve—but he managed to shake different limbs until it fell on all fours with a crash, just as the highway patrol arrived, and he took off.

❋   ❋   ❋   ❋   ❋

And so on a certain July 3, around 4 p.m.—the day is about to become historic—Jesse sits in a doctor's waiting room. Understand that
this is in a small town less than one hundred miles below the Canadian border, and La Chata is pregnant at his elbow. Jesse is turning
through a brochure of baby photos with her, when, for a moment,
he passes through one of those double takes that tuck life into a non-
heroic shape: at age thirty-five, with a pregnant girlfriend, he is dying.
Nothing complicated, stomach cancer, long odds. He holds the photo
album like a steering wheel, and listens to La Chata.

No, the photos aren't of anybody he knows, he tells her. The brochure is nothing but advertising—disposable diapers, bibs, booties—
he explains. And re-explains. *No hay otro.* La Chata is stubborn,
eager to please, away from home for the first time in all of her twenty
chubby years, and wet as the day she was born. Her Ellis Island was
the spare tire in a brother-in-law's trunk.

Six months before, when they met, she kept batting her eyes at the
ground, handshake limp as a poisoned bird. Now she's pregnant, far
from home, and sure his family hates her. Her eyes lead feelings over
her face. She pretends nothing is wrong, but stress leaks out every
which way. She eats ice cream and weeps at her gallstones. She misses
her ride and walks five miles to work. Jesse is truly tired of her—but
even more tired of his own detachment. A stream of wry acknowledg-
ment holds him in place. No wonder they say in el norte your only
companion is the ceiling.

Leaving the doctor's office, Jesse enters oblique, Pacific Northwest
sunlight, and passes pickup loads of Anglo teenagers shirtless with
firecrackers and beer. At a stoplight, on the car radio, when the afternoon becomes historic, Jesse blinks. He imagines the bit of news he
blinks at reaching kitchen tables where mexicano families sit chewing
and nodding: *fíjate*, the PRI lost.

For the first time in seventy-some years, the ruling party has lost a
presidential election in Mexico. Jesse winks at La Chata. Good thing
the locals dedicate tomorrow to roastin' ears and pitchin' horseshoes.

Because here is something to celebrate. Perfect strangers grin at each other across the Safeway beer display—isn't it the damnedest thing? The PRI lost.

Jesse feels a difference in the air, the river, the squat sagebrush hills. What is it? Something is gone—the world looks flatter—everything looks filmed and framed. The green hay acreage, red barns and white clapboard dwellings, the locals blue-eyed and sunburned, and very hard to figure out. Self-conscious? Not them. One walks by looking right through you, her butt peeking out of ragged cutoffs. Another checks his billfold at the sight of you.

The difference is that the PRI lost. Hay crews wear the spacey look of people witnessing what they can't believe. Nobody wants to shower or shoot pool. People collect in threes or fours in trailer shadows. They talk until long after dark, *po's, un tranquilazo*. Either you purr like a radio announcer, or you admit you have no idea what Mexico will look like without the PRI. The hemming and hawing goes on all night, that raised eyebrow migrant mexicanos turn on each other, on the world.

❀   ❀   ❀   ❀   ❀

Born in 1898, the patron saint of illegal immigrants grew up smooth-cheeked and dumpy, with a soprano voice, a harmless eccentric who frequently dressed as the Virgin of Guadalupe. Even in childhood, Niño could read his playmates' minds, a stunt they often rewarded with a thrashing. Grown, he worked preparing medicines from herbs and plants—at least until he underwent some subtle change in his late twenties. By the time of his death, in 1938—many of his followers even now claim the government assassinated him—Niño was Mexico's most famous curandero, or folk healer.

His cult began in a town near Espinazo—writes Prof. Heliodoro Gonzáles Valdés—where there lived a wealthy railroad man whose wife's pregnancy was threatened. After three days, the man sent a handcar for El Niño, who arrived within the hour, and asked for a bottle. He broke it, chose which piece to use, and performed, in an instant, what we call a caesarean. After he removed the infant, dead for three days, and now completely black, the señora recovered, and even had more children. The grateful husband asked Niño how he could ever repay him. "If you would," piped Niño, "I'd like for you to send me back in that same contraption."

Niño spent his whole life in Espinazo. A decade after a civil war that cost a million lives, on the route of what was already a mass migration north, he plied his trade, and became famous. A journalist wrote that he resembled someone who lived out in the rain, extremely pale, deep-sunken eyes, constantly dropping his lower lip to the left, sleeves rolled up. Forever among the sick, forever warning he'd lose his healing power if he experienced sexual pleasure or charged money. And who knows, maybe he suffered some degree of retardation, like people said, not to mention hallucinations.

But Niño always seemed to know exactly what he was doing. His methods? He prescribed cups of herb tea (*gobernadora*) and prayed with those who were gravely ill. Tumors he removed with a piece of glass—even though grateful patients gave him dozens of scalpels—and strangely enough, despite undergoing major surgery with no anaesthetic, his patients reported no pain.

As befits those whose very presence is illegal, who break the law by merely existing somewhere, Niño knows exactly what it is to feel left out: he was never canonized. At least he hasn't been yet. Of course Catholics all over the world lobby for the bestowal of sainthood on local holy people. How many tons of candles are produced every year in the hope of accumulating examples of intercessions by non-canonical figures? At one shrine in Texas, pilgrims light so many votive candles a shrine employee has to cart them to an adjoining room, and visitors are nearly overcome by the heat.

✳   ✳   ✳   ✳   ✳

Nearly anything will work as a votive offering, by the way. Consider the crutches and medical instruments at Lourdes, silver hearts at the Church of the Assumption in London, and wedding rings on the tabernacle-veil of Westminster Cathedral. Think of money pinned to trees at the hillside shrine of St. Michael in Albania, and baby shoes at a shrine in Chimayo, New Mexico. Still, the typical votive offering left in west-central Mexico, a *retablo*, is a painting—on a piece of tin—that measures from six to fifteen inches on a side. Three elements characterize the retablo: the graphic rendering of a miraculous event, a holy image, a text explaining what occurred. Jorge Durand and Douglas Massey write that, with text to narrate the miracle, and the image to identify the benefactor, the rendering nearly always flattens time into a single scene, one with broad compositional features.

In one retablo, M. Esther Tapia Picón finds herself, while trying to cross the border, kneeling behind a single green bush in a huge, flat, coconut-colored desert. Off in the distance, two tiny blue-uniformed figures stand beside a crudely drawn yellow van, lettering tiny on one side, *p-o-l-i l*, a wheel well cutting off the rest. A Los Angeles city limits sign appears to the right of them, and to their left, dangling mirage-style midair, a handful of skyscrapers and tiny clouds, to indicate how close María Esther is to a whole new life, as she crouches behind that bush. Level with the Virgin's image, a desert-colored helicopter hangs in the over-blue sky. Out of that black doorway, shrinking day and night to a single moment, a spotlight beam probes the ground.

❊   ❊   ❊   ❊   ❊

Jesse loved to recall his own good luck the first time he crossed. Age sixteen, getting off a bus in Tijuana with five pesos, he met some other guys and set out for San Diego. But over the first hill, a car pulled up with two *judiciales*, who started pocketing people's money. "How much you gonna chip in, asshole?" they said to Jesse. "*Compa*"— picture him turning both palms up—"gimme a break, I only got five pesos." "*Cinco pinches pesos,*" the officer rolled his eyes. "¡*Píntate!* Get outa here!" Six hours later Jesse was picking California oranges.

It was twenty years later when Jesse—having meanwhile acquired a green card and stomach cancer—swore he'd to live to see his baby walk, a vow that got him six weeks of chemo, followed by surgery to remove three-quarters of his stomach. But after two months La Chata—he later explained to the landlady—had stood as much as she could, and lit out for her parents' place in California. She bundled the baby, and climbed on one of those hundred-dollar Golden State busses. It was January, and snowing. Jesse waved goodbye at the tinted window, drove home, took two hits of morphine, and slept twelve hours.

But sure enough, on a follow-up trek to the radiation lab, Jesse knuckled tears out of his eyes and hiccupped. He wanted La Chata to come back on the next bus and act like she loved him. He wanted her, right down to the Bi-Mart apple-shampoo scent when she closed the door. The steamy-bathroom routine. And wanting someone that much trained an itchy perspective on your whole existence, no? Beyond the aches and urges accumulated in twenty years of packing shed shifts and trailer-court weekends—life framed by space heater, ice chest—guys like Jesse flew back and forth, until they hit some inner limit, and hit hard. A fixed expiration date? Sure he felt cornered. But the main surprise—he closed his eyes—was the lack of urgency, the damn near gleeful calm.

La Chata came back, and then she left again. Various times in fact. And every time, the day she left, the same neighbor lady moved in with Jesse, a heavyset mother of four—left her kids back in Guadalajara—who finally got her own heart broken when Jesse fled to Idaho with that fourteen-year-old niece he got pregnant.

❖   ❖   ❖   ❖   ❖

How do Mexican intellectuals see the Niño Cult? Carlos Monsiváis called it an exercise in the mystique of the margins—a new syncretistic tradition combining *curanderismo* with spiritualism, Catholicism of the masses with pilgrimage as an end in itself. Even those who identify very different ingredients agree with Monsiváis on one point: Niño was the kind of charismatic personality who, intentionally or not, is used to filter religious experience.

Which is to say that, right from the start, Niño was a symbol. He filtered the experience of a people hoodwinked by history, *los brinca-alambres*, or border hoppers, the mexicano migrant poor—people for whom the cult was already well established by February 1928, when El Niño received a visit from President Calles himself. The press coverage that resulted joined them forever after in popular thinking: Nino's blank look vs. that square-jaw politician's eyes, hooded, reflective, predatory.

Born in Sonora, nicknamed El Turco for what were apparently Lebanese immigrant grandparents, Calles became a schoolteacher and Marxist, then a soldier and president. February 1928 saw him finishing his masterwork: the coalition—prototype of the PRI—that historians sixty years later would call the most successful political party of the twentieth century. It imposed a federal *pax romana*, which in turn produced—in the 1970s, before the peso crashed—what more than one economist hailed as the Mexican Miracle.

The day he visited Niño, Calles had one eye on history. And why not? To that inventory of lethal and wide-eyed expressions the twentieth century began with—Proletarian Revolution, "War to End All Wars"—Mexico's contributions would be unambiguous as a pick handle: *tierra y libertad*, and *sufragio efectivo/no reelección*. Otherwise though, while the Revolution petered out, the PRI tinkered with land reform. And Mexico's government by the end of the century? In Jesse's trailer court, the night the PRI was voted out, when several generations of people agreed it was nothing but Leninist opportunism blended with Aztec logic, the last bit of the Mexican Miracle collapsed.

Calles was maybe the most bull-headed Mexican president ever. Assuming office, as he did, after a bloodbath civil war had reduced the country's population by ten percent, another president might have set out uniting factions, compromising, negotiating. But not Plutarco Elías Calles. A militant atheist, he ramrodded anti-clerical legislation so blunt it was clear he meant to eliminate the Catholic Church as a power in national life, and soon found himself suppressing a major rebellion, La Cristiada. The Calles government's inventory of church goods was the last straw—writes historian Jean Meyer—and riots broke out all over the west-central highlands. A spasm of lynchings, firing squads, ambushes, and half-planned assaults prompted Calles to respond with more than one hundred thousand troops and a gruesome counter-insurgency campaign. Calles's *intrasigence*, in the end, cost a quarter of a million Mexican lives.

His visit to El Niño, therefore, represents a curious gap in the President's anti-clerical zeal. Was it only a matter of public relations? What inner voices made Calles ignore the pleading of his doctors, the counsel of his advisors, and drop in on Niño to get treated for what, some say, was a skin rash? They spent six hours together. Nobody has the least idea what happened. Only that Niño gave him a cup of tea brewed from roses and honey, and rubbed a soap-and-tomato potion on him. Presidential aides forbade photographs of course. Even so, the two remain paired in popular thinking—the greatest church-hater in Mexican history and his token holy man.

We have to imagine that moment when the dying Revolution made its awkward, ad hoc, and very ambiguous peace with God. Calles would have found Niño in a small theater, surrounded by various pretty women dressed in white. Waiting next door to be operated on, a patient surrounded by thirty jars of tumors Niño recently had removed. Probably the tour proceeded then to the *círculo*, a kind of hut, where Fidencio did general curing. Beyond lay a delivery room full of women who had given birth the day before. And out the door, in a cage, the panther (teeth and claws removed) that he used to treat the mute—he said the fear cured them.

Niño was at his most picturesque when treating the mad. But who knows whether President Calles saw him seat a couple of poor demented souls in swings and then, when they least expected, pelt them with oranges, hard, smack. An immediate effect of the presidential visit was that Niño's fame grew and grew. Soon unable to treat individuals, he was reduced to performing mass cures from the roof of his house, throwing oranges at the crowd. Whoever was hit by one was cured.

❊   ❊   ❊   ❊   ❊

Jesse's luck ran out in Idaho. First, it became hard to swallow. With a sprained-ankle wince, he picked at a cheeseburger, broke a french fry in half. Day by day, tinier bites, till he quit eating in front of people. Within a month, he was getting down only those cans of sweet goo the doctor recommended. Bones showed through his face and arms, and specialists were all over him. MRIs, CAT scans, he must have drunk gallons of barium. The specialists were baffled, threw up their hands, guessed it was scar tissue from his surgery—so Jesse quit going for checkups. He lived on goo and beer.

But that diet furnished energy enough for him to give convention one final, sincere nose-thumbing. A lot of people said what Jesse did exposed the selfish and irresponsible side of guys like him. It certainly got everybody's attention. The niece he fell in love with *was* fourteen— he never denied it—but not a blood relative, only a sister-in-law's daughter by a previous marriage. Anyhow, this Carla, a pretty kid, had showed up at his brother's house with blisters on her feet from one of those post–September 11 marathon border crossings. She slept three days and nights, then woke and shaved her legs and bought a bra.

She borrowed a library card and brought home volumes of poetry and science fiction. But no, she didn't want to finish school. Seizing her stepfather's Spanish-English dictionary, she studied Help Wanted ads, found work sorting potatoes, and arranged a ride to work. She decided her stepfather's brother Jesse was very nice, and hormones did the rest. In a couple of weeks, when somebody phoned the authorities, the happy couple beat it across the Idaho line.

But don't get me wrong. No miraculous intervention whatever saved Jesse. Maybe Niño had sponsored his life, but Jesse's departure from it was all his own. Having outlived the PRI, and dodged Child Protective Services, he heard a Boise doctor describe the tumors that wrapped his esophagus like a vine. He hunkered down for five weeks of anticlimax, vomiting buckets of blood in a studio apartment. Then he was dead.

❊   ❊   ❊   ❊   ❊

How does popular thinking decide that X is the patron saint of Y? Overlapping interests count for a lot. Recalling the classical Greek gods, who tended to sponsor people who reminded them of themselves, it's no surprise to learn that public relations experts are in the hands of St. Paul, nor that the snake-bitten pray to St. Patrick, although the latter does get toothache cases as well. Sponsorship apparently can get very specific. Sufferers from gout and lumbago and breast cancer pray to particular saints, as do cabdrivers and grave diggers, milliners and leather workers, paratroopers and plasterers and pawnbrokers, air travelers and amputees, kidnap victims and TV personalities.

Niño is patron of lives like Jesse's, however, because of how the faithful depend on him. While it is true that surgery patients, before going under, commend themselves to the Infant of Prague, mexicano migrants count on Niño in a very different way, one apparent only over time. Niño offers neither protection nor care nor nurturing, only clarity of purpose. Look at how he lived, after all. Money, fruit, foods, jewelry, any distraction the faithful brought him, he pitched it to the crowd from his roof. It wasn't a few Stephen Spielberg cures, in other words, that made that town grow up around him. Because stubborn, hopeless people kept showing up to observe other stubborn, hopeless people, Niño became patron of perseverance. Tuberculosis and cancer victims, lepers, psychotics, do-gooders and legless beggars, everybody agreed.

In retrospect, Monsiváis offers a level-headed analysis: Niño worship seems to posit a world of parallel events, one in which hair-raising partnerships thrive, and bitter contraries cuddle up lion-and-lamb style. The cult is a product, he argues, of people's faith in the link between everyday life and liturgy's representations of the otherworldly. Treat your life as a pilgrimage, Monsiváis concludes, and yes, the world will appear all heaven, hell and limbo, virgins and apparitions and miracles, possessions both satanic and seraphic. Acting like life is a pilgrimage condemns you to live in a retablo, a world without secular features—an existence the level-headed flinch at.

Of course, the level-headed also flinch when the faithful channel Niño. And yet, we want to ask, who doesn't share the occasional hunch that somebody else's speech, or part of it at least, has origins beyond the here and now, and authority to match? It certainly isn't news that opportunists like Calles, rational folk with tight ego boundaries, contaminate the faith of others. By channeling Niño, the faithful keep their lives open to a kind of spirit-ventriloquism. Because it is a practice they share, at one remove or another, with nearly everyone else, Niño tells them that time is their only weapon.

12   The Unforgettable Frozen Chicken Giveaway and What Came After

1.

They're anything but hapless masses herded across the border, the mexicanos who visit our food bank. Their presence here in the Inland Empire is voluntary, to say the least. Knowing they'll be a long way from home, exposed to the least twitch in weather systems, in international prices, they show up, and hang on. They live on a margin too thin to permit an excess of anything but a certain kind of laughter—the corrosive, liberating stuff that keeps you alive.

My friends Irma and Beto and I barely knew each other, ten years ago, when we agreed to distribute surplus food that came free from a warehouse in Yakima. But over the past ten years, while filling out so many forms that we got each others' dates of birth and Social Security numbers memorized, we've come to share the oblique stuff that people who have to trust each other share: peeves and recurring dreams, allergies, saints' days. For a while, tongue in cheek, we even addressed each other, Cuban-style, as *compañero*. By now we find our feelings for those we serve and for each other equally binding, intimate but not intrusive, and necessary, truly necessary.

A blend of the comic and urgent took over the very first time we three compañeros distributed food. It was mid-June when the County Action Council phoned in a panic. They had to get rid of twenty boxes of frozen chickens, stuff that had started to thaw when something malfunctioned. Irma made some phone calls, Beto gave a few rides, and less than an hour later one hundred families stood at the Council's front door, everybody flat broke, and it was dinner time.

Beto had ten boxes stacked before the crowd arrived. Now he pirouetted a hand truck into place with the last ten boxes. When Irma lifted her ballpoint pen to start taking names, Beto opened the top box, and then stood there blinking. The ten chickens in the box had half thawed and then refrozen. Now they glommed each other in what looked—except for the ice—like a raw, pink, chicken-orgy enthusiasm. Imagine a creature all elbows and goose bumps. Those chickens clutched each other so tight you couldn't break them apart—maybe with a hammer, but forget it.

"We better distribute this stuff a box at a time," Irma decided. "Five families to a box," Beto called out to people waiting in line.

And so we brought it off. But talk about a conflict of perspectives. Because from perspective #1, the public driving by notices whole households nodding thanks, calling back over one shoulder, "que dios se lo pague." But then perspective #2, a close-up, reveals those very same mexicanos shrugging, elbowing each other. "¿Y para quebrar esta paleta de pollo?" This chickensicle—how you bust it up?

Note the difference. Try to measure the distance. Perspective #1, the panning shot, shows the grateful poor getting fed like sheep, while #2, the close-up, reveals the same people, nonplused but nonchalant, strolling off as if they were used to getting handed twenty-five pound lumps of frozen chicken. While each is accurate, as far as it goes, the two perspectives are truly incompatible. What does it matter that both versions really exist? They do so in different mental time zones. Mutual invisibility nearly guarantees the result. They're sealed off from each other by traffic patterns of thought, speech, habit.

And Los Tres Compañeros? We marveled at how far it was from one perspective to the other. Even after we got to feeling like veteran commuters, the view remained breathtaking. Part of the closeness we shared owed to our constantly negotiating hairpin curves of culture, family, language. We've secured space in the old boiler plant of the local university by now, but all three of us still believe that the comic and the urgent do balance. Though sometimes, we admit, you have to wonder.

2.

A middle-aged man with a quiet voice, with searching, deliberate speech patterns, compañero Beto climbs behind the steering wheel and closes the door. It is bright and windy. Compañero Beto is setting out to visit campsites and trailer courts up and down the river. He and I plan a laid-back day of taping flyers to Laundromat windows, of shaking hands and hanging out, of hearing the same old stories about poor people a long way from home, tales that feature the athlete's-foot optimism of immigrant life.

Beto hasn't worked in five years. He no longer needs the crutches he used when he fell off a ladder, twelve feet onto concrete, and lit on the small of his back. But anybody can see that his body still rings like a bell. He crosses his kitchen floor with icy-sidewalk steps. The soles of his feet burn and itch, he says. Even now, he dreams he is falling, and wakes with his back knotted.

It was four years ago that a balding Anglo doctor confessed, with sad eyes, to seeing nothing in X-rays to account for the pain that threw a person breathless on the couch after five minutes of dish washing, the cramps that climbed both shoulder blades when lifting a gallon of milk. Ever since the week he was hurt, Beto's family has lived off what his wife earns by cleaning rooms at a freeway-exchange motel, a drab, two-story job that sits downwind from a feeder lot.

Beto's days shrink with chores like driving his children to school, patching window screens, plucking trash from the gravel paths that wind through the trailer court out his window. Day after day at the kitchen table, with a lunch box full of unpaid bills, his chainsaw and hard hat and boots in a pile at the back door, pruning shears rusting in the pickup bed, his only relief has been this: leafleting and listening, campfire to convenience store, pool hall to Laundromat to auto parts. Up and down the banks of either river—Yakima or Columbia—hard-luck stories fly like pollen.

We're down the road. An oily rainbow straddles the freeway entrance, sagebrush whips by, and the pickup motor whines. At the tip of a phone pole, a hawk looks like something stamped on a coin.

Gulleys, gulches, dry washes, and ravines—and then, at Ryegrass, the land dips toward the river. Seagulls perch on a bridge girder.

Sagebrush, small town. One more peeling Sumercado sign. When Beto thumbtacks a flyer to the bulletin board, a teenager sidles up in denim jacket and baseball cap. "Don Beto, buenas tardes . . . Disculpe la molestia, es que venía pidiendo una cooperación. . . ."

The youngster is raising money to ship what is left of a run-over uncle back to get buried in Uruapan. Beto hands him a dollar, then asks the young fellow how he himself is bearing up. "¿Yo? ¿Cómo estoy aguantando? Pos' la mera verdad, yo ando más aguamiel que pulque." The kids fights tears. Beto listens, equal parts reserve and resolve.

This happens a lot. Troubled, frightened, injured, strangers appear out of nowhere to talk to my friend Beto. He doesn't appear to say much, but people respond to his light, fluid touch, *la política de escuchar al callado*. A politics of listening to people who don't talk much.

By late afternoon, re-crossing the bridge, the sagebrush a horizontal streak, Beto is recalling that his life on this side of the border dates from 1978, the year when thugs of a newly imposed governor back in Guerrero nabbed his uncle. When a neighbor knocked at the door one afternoon, he and his aunt and his mother raced to the jail.

"Uncle Isaac never had a chance," Beto says. "The cops hated him. He was the kind of guy who settled any dispute at night on back roads."

"We hurried around back to the squad room. Just in time to see him pitched into a car trunk. My aunt turned to *el comandante*—who surely would have the goodness to spare a poor man's life, would he not?"

"What did the guy say?"

"Nothing. You know when time slows down? She kept repeating the same words, but after a while her voice was squeaking."

"Squeaking?"

"*Crujía*. Think how you cut a cardboard box."

"¿Y el comandante?"

"Finally the comandante shrugged, and the car drove off."

"What did you do?"

"Well, neither the lawyer we hired nor the judge we bribed found out a thing. So we held a month-long vigil. Right in front of city hall."

"Did it make any difference?"

"Sort of. One day when I got off my shift at the gasworks, I found two guys in loose-fitting shirts waiting out front. When they followed me in a tinted-windshield SUV without license plates, I bought a pistol, and hid out in my sister's house for three months. Finally, I figured I better head north."

And that is absolutely all. Beto has nothing more to say about how he got here. The rest of it isn't worth talking about, he says. More questions evoke only a low hiss and backward flick of one hand—the gesture with which a sidewalk vendor waves off mention of imperfections in detail.

The hiss-and-flick dismissal is really a mexicano default setting, a southpaw subjunctive, a high sign acknowledging and dismissing whatever triggers it. It is neither admission nor denial. Not even *no comment*. After thirty seconds of silence, Beto changes the subject.

"Hear about don Raúl and his church?"

"You mean that congregation out on Sixteenth Avenue?"

"That very outfit."

"Well, I know he attends Mass there, has for a couple years. Except when he goes back to Oaxaca."

"*Pues, fíjate*, last winter in Oaxaca, his wife died, *la pobrecita*. So he got some maestro back there to make him a Virgen. Wanted to commemorate his wife."

"Uh-oh."

"With all the clothing, the detail work, it set him back a thousand, maybe more."

"And I suppose he donates La Virgen to that Yakima congregation he worships with?"

"Of course he does."

The pickup finally slips through a cut bank, down toward the streetlights, seven hundred feet below, where we live.

"So how long did that arrangement last?"

"It was a couple of months before a janitor broke the news to him. Turned out La Virgen sat on the altar only during the mass they said in Spanish. Otherwise, they kept her in a broom closet."

The gesture makes a big difference. Who knows why it works? You make a sound like a tire losing air, you raise one hand slow motion, like drawing burned fingers back, and life goes on without interruption.

3.

A bronze plaque on one wall says the boiler plant dates from 1947, but it feels independent of time. Here I am deep in the guts of a state institution, huge maroon vats and sheet-metal ducts, and shadows that never move—nothing to suggest all those weather-swings out the door, the turnover rate of heat and cold, plant life and human life.

The chocolate-colored floor tiles and walls of rust-red brick are absorbing light. The cream-colored plaster ceiling, twelve feet high, holds a single seventy-five-watt bulb every twenty feet. Up and down the corridor, from first-aid kit to water cooler, from the door entitled Carpentry Shop to the cork board labeled Union News—everything smells like floor wax and disinfectant applied right on schedule, year after year, by nameless guys with state jobs.

Out the room's single window lies a foreground of juniper bed, the high-rise dormitories and parking lot of a regional university, then a spruce-bough horizon, a shortgrass ridge. Between the boughs and the ridge—you can't see it from here—the Yakima River twists down through basalt canyons and into the open.

It is 9 a.m. I get a kick out of putting in hours with Irma on these quiet weekday mornings. Her attitude always picks me up. Feisty, tireless, with a long memory and a short temper, she is a dear and squirmy friend, nettlesome but cuddly, exasperated, exasperating. She opens an Exacto knife, and cuts a fifty-pound sack of masa, and seizes a half-gallon plastic scoop. I spread open a Ziploc bag and, oops, spilled masa clouds the room. Irma sneezes.

"Salud."

She blows her nose in a wadded Kleenex.

"Gracias."

Urgency sharpens her voice. Gotta be the stress of being a single mother, of caring for invalids three nights a week to pay rent. Of average height, slender, with short hair, she wears sensible shoes. Her eyes are large and far apart and expressive. She could run you out of a room with those eyes.

We met six years ago. "What a grim sense of humor God has"— she said over restaurant coffee—"stranding us here among a bunch of people every bit as stubborn as we are." She was straightforward about how she needed to serve the mexicano community. "Mi pasión es el trabajo social."

Irma is, first, a survivor—if only because her own mood changes are part of what she has to survive. Her life takes demanding angles: six kids and a couple of husbands, and then, twelve years ago, moving three thousand miles north to a new life in the Yakima River watershed. She veers from resentful to adulatory and back in one warp-accelerated moment, from growly to giddy, from pouring out her heart to issuing airy denials. But when shy newcomers cluster at the food bank door, a circus-barker note enters her voice. She calms the timid with the tone of a droll emcee at a bingo parlor, a sidewalk *varillero* vending powders and snakeskin.

Like few people I know, she has created herself. She radiates a willfulness of the most basic kind. It luxuriates in its own reversibility. Smart and easily bored, she has uncanny recall for details, but forgets to fill out her time sheets. Her tones change in a gear too low to be heard by the human ear. When caught between two of her feelings, I think of how local walls growl from over-stressed basalt one hundred miles away.

And yet, because I see a lot of what happens to me as an accident, a minor dust-up at the intersection of Comic and Urgent, I zoom in on the conflict of perspectives the three of us generated that afternoon we gave away the chickens. It is obvious, in retrospect: the three of us struck a deal. Somehow, we gave each other the high sign, and started trusting—each drawn to the other two by something like the mutual flinch that binds those who survive the same earthquake or flood.

What we survived was a mexicano invasion. I recall how local Anglos stared, years ago, when the first families arrived. Teenage *mexicanas* got so tired of remarks about having *the prettiest hair*, while their mothers learned to ignore the supermarket checkout-line double takes—at someone buying tripe, not ground beef, limes instead of lemons. Life became pretty intricate for a while. Any bag boy who ever took a year of high-school Spanish wanted to see if the stuff really worked.

And yet, over time, the steady arrival of immigrants has had a broad, subtle effect on immigrant life. Before long, the newly arrived become a yardstick, a way to measure how well it is that you yourself have acclimated. Still, no matter how relative the status of *newcomer*, when the newly arrived observe the even more newly arrived, they see a rawer, purer version of themselves, an opportunistic innocent baffled by electric garage doors, by garbage compactors and answering machines.

I represent a very different perspective. What I represent is a build-up, something like metal fatigue, the basic friction between specifics and staying power. Employed for thirty-five years at the local seat of higher learning, I grumble as much as I did when I arrived here about the weather—which is to say, about life itself—specifically about the various tricks of wind and sunlight that pass for a climate here. Talk about unpredictable. Not to mention heavy-handed, unruly, even vindictive. Everybody knows that Badger Pocket ranchers have a growing season ten days shorter than neighbors one hundred feet lower. Or is that Hungry Junction ranchers?

There's a wind, year-round, monotonous. It forms the only constant in a valley otherwise all aftereffects: drought or blizzard, flood or forest fire. A light snowpack dries up reservoirs and wilts corn, one year, and the next, half an hour of hail trashes a cherry crop. And yet, if the climate cuts ranchers and farmers very little slack, it is even more demanding on the mexicano families who show up to work—in warehouses, in fields and orchards, in one of five county plants that press timothy hay, in the local freezer plant. Mexicanos arrived here so fast that, by the end of the twentieth century, more than a thousand of them depended on a makeshift food bank in a back room on the university campus. It is where Irma and I are bagging food this morning.

The people who receive the food will show up in rusted pickup-camper combos, or gas guzzlers twenty years old with bald tires. They are the kind of folks who pull into town, reach behind spare tire or toolbox, pull out trash bags stuffed with clothing and change clothes, eat a sandwich, and hunt work. Many show up not expecting to stay, though some in fact find year-round work. They stay at least long enough to watch their kids board a yellow school bus and come home speaking unaccented English. Even with twenty people sleeping in shifts in a two-bedroom trailer, even sleeping under plastic tarps in a rest area, the newly arrived keep reassuring each other—*ni modo, que uno se acostumbra*—that yes, you really do get accustomed to life here.

Anyhow, ten years into the project, with perspectives still accumulating, the same old sunlight inches across the floor. It is a weekday morning. Compañeros Irma and Felipe do battle with half a ton of rice and beans. Two and a half scoops to a bag. Eighteen bags to a shelf.

4.

Every September, people get together on Mexican Independence Day to do a year's worth of unwinding. One particular year, Irma obtained permission to celebrate at the Catholic church, and the three of us drove downriver to buy a pig. It must've been the year the Princess of Wales died in a wreck. I remember Irma rolling her eyes when the televised flowers hit that televised hearse.

In a taco truck at an intersection, where we stopped to ask directions, a heavyset señora dabbed her eyes and chopped parsley, a TV set at her elbow. "La pobrecita. . . ." We stood there and shook our heads. Sliding off a black fender, flowers yellow, white, pink. La señora blew her nose, and pointed down the road at a corner.

Beto turned at that corner, and parked by a corrugated metal roof nailed over 2x4's, shading sweet corn and cantaloupe, honeydew and

watermelon, tomato and tomatillo and jalapeño, stuff plucked from
fields so level they broke only at willow lines where the creeks flowed.
We shook hands with four *ancianitos*—senior citizens missing teeth,
gray-haired, in T-shirts and huaraches. The guys had installed two
living-room couches under a tree, and strung up a tarp, and nailed a
hammock in the shade. Now they were presiding over tons of produce,
not to mention a pen of pigs and goats. Innumerable grandsons and
nephews jumped at every nod and monosyllable the guys emitted.

Our wad of bills vanished, and a glance sent a sow to her death.
She collapsed on a plywood slab on the ground, and knives freed the
hide from fat snick-snick. I kept swiping my baseball cap at chickens
that gathered, fluttered away, re-gathered.

❊   ❊   ❊   ❊   ❊

Beto drove to the Cascade Way Mobile Home Park, to the trailer of
don Raúl, who produced a propane burner and a big, hammered-
copper *cazo*. He started the *chicharrones* sizzling, and then added a
gallon of lard, salt and pepper, a bottle of Coca-Cola, a stream of Pet
Milk. He stirred it all with a piece of lath, and sat on a kitchen chair,
and twisted a beer open.

"Today she would've turned sixty."

I flinched. Don Raúl was still recalling how hard his wife fought
cancer before she died. Beto and I studied the lumps of pork bubbling
at our feet.

Eulogizing a wife who struggled so long that her medical bills
finally cost him all three houses he owned, plus his butcher shop, don
Raúl's voice never broke. "¡Cómo aguantaba!" Her capacity for dis-
comfort—no two ways about it—he admired the staying power that
left him in exile in el norte working for minimum wage.

Producing a pair of tongs, don Raúl began plucking squares of
pork from the cazo. As if to change the subject, he cleared his throat.
He seemed to be choosing his words.

"That princess on TV"—no expression whatever crossed his
face—"she died fleeing photographers, not cops, not even migra."

Beto and I were wrapping pork in tinfoil. Don Raúl smiled and let the irony build. I was ready for him to contrast the flowers sliding off the princess's hearse with the weedy plot his wife lay in. Ironies bristled all around us. I expected a dose of that numinous itching powder people call *belonging*. But no, the words he finally uttered were nothing special at all, except of course for their tone: dense with grief, ventilated with wry asides, a tone enough at ease with itself to append the moral that all our lives are in God's hands *ni más ni menos*.

❆   ❆   ❆   ❆   ❆

By 8 p.m., in the church basement, teenagers had the rug rolled up, and the *banda* music throbbing. Grasping each other at arm's length, boys and girls danced with loping, determined strides. In straight-back chairs, dressed in black, grandmothers and widowed aunts let fly with commentary behind one hand. Under a bunch of Kmart red and green and white balloons, Beto and Irma stood slicing pork onto paper plates.

That was when Irma cleared her throat, and asked point blank, "¿Qué tal eso de los pollos, los congelados?"

I gave her a blank look.

"I mean, you know, *aquel bisnes* that you, our chronicler, El Maestro Felipe . . . anyhow you said you were going to put all this in a book that you were writing."

"Oh. That."

"Said you meant to call it—that chapter about the food bank—'The Unforgettable Frozen Chicken Giveaway of August '95.'"

"Ya estuvo," I sniffed. Already got it written up, thank you.

Although that wasn't the truth. Not at all. What I didn't tell La Compañera was that, well, I continued juggling perspectives. It wasn't easy to find the right wide-angle blend of tones to register the feelings my friends underwent this far from home.

It came down to this: no matter what, they couldn't dodge a phrase that they themselves used to describe what was, at once, the best and the worst of each other—*el pinche mexicano*. You heard it everywhere, that phrase, followed by a head-shake, to indicate extremes—to indicate great excess, whether of self-sacrifice or greed, of willpower or apathy. And the attitude or conduct in question? It might inspire or dismay the head-shaker, but either way—swallow-flight triumph, or dog-shit shame—what was being acknowledged was a collective appreciation of excess, and therefore of limits. A 90-year-old woman getting married, a teenager returning from Iraq with a Purple Heart—mexicanos shook their heads at all that people just like them were capable of. That was when you heard the phrase *el pinche mexicano* take on life. It could turn self-parody to fighting words in milliseconds. It exposed a state of mind cursed and blessed and truly indelible.

As mexicanos talked to each other about el pinche mexicano, stories overlapped, and a caricature wiggled free, an authentic folklore phantom, a rhetoric trajectory. El pinche mexicano rebounded from one role to another—passerby, butt of jokes, holy fool. One tale had a whole family lying still as quail in long grass by a freeway, the boots of the migra so close they smelled the shoe polish.

As daily life condensed, then evaporated, el pinche mexicano became the offspring of asymmetries, of traits arbitrarily linked, the hybrid of stereotype and observation that flashed through mexicanos when observing each other. Scrawny, with quick wits, 35 percent sense of humor by body weight, forever either too proud or too meek, improvident but tough, a songbird of a person, someone that worked insanely hard. With an address written in ink on one palm, el pinche mexicano navigated unpronounceable place names. And, therefore, was invoked wherever people sat down to unwind over stories about how out of place a person felt, how isolated. After all, there were only ties of blood and marriage and time—mainly of time—binding people one hundred miles apart into a neighborhood, a net of needs and memories two days' drive from the Mexican border.

But writing about el pinche mexicano was tricky. Noting in English what stuff happened to my friends was easy. What was hard was registering the tone of voice they reacted to it in. English had no equivalent, no counterpart to a very specific attitude my friends aimed at each other. You simply could not make English make the sound that came from don Raúl when he spoke of life in the United States.

And I was out to catch that tone, the attitude my friends responded with—not to migrant life, but rather to what had become a de facto exile. Everybody agreed: after September 11, 2001, Border Patrol surveillance intensified so much that would-be illegal aliens, merely to get across the border, had to hire a professional guide, some *pollero* or *coyote* to lead them on three- and four-day treks through the desert. It cost about $2,500 a head to be smuggled across the border nowadays. Migrants like don Raúl became immigrants. Without the money to visit hometown and family, immigrants quit talking about home, or mentioned it with resentment. They felt they fit in nowhere, trapped between one landscape and another, a history as random as that set of volcanic high-jinks we call the horizon.

OK, if I wanted to feature the tough glee my friends treated each other with, their calculated merriment, how about recalling the time that four of them opened a restaurant in the spirit of *empresarios*—plus how they went broke in the spirit of St. Lawrence asking the Roman torturer searing his flesh to flip him, hamburger-style. Tough glee it was, OK, but with a warning label. If mexicanos received frustration or disappointment with what sounded, when put into English, like blunt fatalism, it wasn't because they saw themselves as victims. They saw themselves, on the contrary, as part of a boisterous, highly verbal community, one with a set of cliches to be shared, antique expressions to be maintained.

Life was heirloom figures of speech that came with a built-in tone of voice, in short. Whatever kind of book I wrote, attitude would matter more than people's poses, or their candor. Bus station–snapshot lives like those of José and Jesse—and in that same, corner-of-the-mouth tone of voice, centerfold composites named Alma and Lalo, Arturo, Nieves.

One thing I didn't know beforehand, though. I had no idea el pinche mexicano in me, at book's end, would want—no, would outright demand!—to dwell on the sorry finish of our Independence celebration. Years later, it's easy to speak of a glaring imprudence on the part of us three compañeros. Call it a blithe lack of foresight, but taking a certain, simple precaution never occurred to us. After all, sooner or later, one of that pack of kids howling through the halls was sure to yank a fire alarm.

The sound was unearthly. A huge mechanical grinding shook the walls, a racket that swallowed the voices of people five feet away. Penetrating, abrasive, it grated every bit of inflection from Irma's follow-up question about my book. Finally she threw up her hands, and Beto dialed 911, but the Fire Department said to phone the parish.

After maybe twenty minutes, a priest with a trench coat over pajamas stepped through a side door, and flipped a switch, and quiet settled like parachute silk. The priest glanced around, and his eyeglasses became dark. Everybody knew exactly what that fellow wanted to say—something about thick makeup and greasy food, something about your accent and your mustache. Even though all he did was shrug and walk off, he definitely had the look of a guy ready to run somebody naked out of paradise.

WORKS CONSULTED

2000 Census. Washington, D.C.: U.S. Census Bureau, 2000.

Anzaldúa, Gloria. *Borderlands*. San Francisco: Aunt Lute Press, 1999.

Augustín Ramírez, José. *Tragicomedia mexicana 1: La vida de 1940 a 1970*. Espejo de México series. México City: Planeta, 1994.

———. *Tragicomedia mexicana 2: La vida de 1970 a 1982*. Espejo de México series. México City: Planeta, 1996.

———. *Tragicomedia mexicana 3: La vida de 1982 a 1994*. Espejo de México series. México City: Planeta, 1998.

Bodeen, Jim, ed. *Impulse to Love*. Yakima, WA: Blue Begonia Press, 1998.

———. *Seeking Light in Each Dark Room/Buscando luz en cada cuarto oscuro*. Yakima, WA: Blue Begonia Press, 2002.

———. *This House*. Walla Walla, WA: Tsunami Press, 1999.

———. *With My Hands Full/Con mis manos llenas*. Yakima, WA: Blue Begonia Press, 1991.

Bonfil Batalla, Guillermo. *Mexico Profundo: Reclaiming a Civilization*. Trans. Philip A. Dennis. Austin: University of Texas Press, 2001.

Carrillo Strong, Arturo. *Corrido de Cocaine: Inside Stories of Hard Drugs, Big Money and Short Lives*. Tucson, AZ: Harbinger, 1990.

Carvajal Silva, María Raquel, Víctor M. Espinosa Aguilar, Enrique Martínez Curiel and Hugo Velázquez Villa. *El norte es como el mar: Entrevistas a trabajadores migrantes en Estados Unidos*. Ed. Jorge Durand. Guadalajara: Prensa de la Universidad de Guadalajara, 1996.

Castañeda, Jorge G. La herencia: *Arqueología de la sucesión presidencial en México*. Mexico City: Extra Alfaguara, 1999.

Conover, Ted. *Coyotes: A Journey through the Secret World of America's Illegal Aliens.* New York: Vintage Books, 1987.

Corona Núñez, José. *Mitología Tarasca.* Colección Cultural 4. Morelia, Mich.: Secretaría de Educación Pública, 1986.

Davidson, Miriam. *Lives on the Line: Dispatches from the U.S.–Mexico Border.* Tucson: University of Arizona Press, 2000.

Díaz, May N. *Tonalá: Conservatism, Responsibility, and Authority in a Mexican Town.* Berkeley: University of California Press, 1970.

Durán, Diego. *Book of the Gods and Rites and the Ancient Calendar.* Trans. and Ed. Fernando Horcasitas and Doris Heyden. Norman: University of Oklahoma Press, 1971.

Durand, Jorge. *Los obreros de Río Grande.* Zamora: El Colegio de Michoacán, 1996.

——— and Douglas S. Massey. *Miracles on the Border: Retablos of Mexican Migrants to the United States.* Tucson: University of Arizona Press, 1995.

El Niño Fidencio Research Project. 2004. University of Texas at Brownsville. <http://vpea.utb.edu/elnino/> 3 Feb. 2005.

Espín Díaz, Jaime L. *Tierra fría: Tierra de conflictos en Michoacán.* Zamora: El Colegio de Michoacán, 1986.

Fonseca, Omar. "Don Manuel: Historia de un migrante." *Boletín del Centro de Estudios de la Revolución Mexicana.* July 1986: 25–114.

Foster, George M. *Tzintzuntzan: Mexican Peasants in a Changing World.* Little, Brown Series in Anthropology. Boston: Little, Brown, 1967.

Gamboa, Erasmo. *Mexican Labor and World War II: Braceros in the Pacific Northwest, 1942–1947.* Austin: University of Texas Press, 1990.

Gamio, Manuel. *The Mexican Immigrant.* 1931. New York: Arno, 1969.

González González, José. *Lo negro del negro Durazo.* 8th ed. Mexico: Editorial Posada, 1983.

Guzik, David. "Luke 2: Jesus' Birth and Boyhood." "Commentaries." *Enduring Word Media.* 2000. <http://www.enduringword.com/com mentaries/4202.htm> 3 Feb. 2005.

Hernández Venegas, Rogelio. "El desarrollo de capitalismo y la urbanización de Morelia, 1940–1980." *Urbanización y Desarrollo en Mi-*

choacán. Ed. Gustavo López Castro. Zamora: El Colegio de Michoacán, 1991. 261–86.

Herrera-Sobek, María. *The Mexican Corrido: A Feminist Analysis.*
Bloomington: Midland–Indiana University Press, 1993.

Iglesias, Norma. *La flor más bella de la maquiladora: Historias de vida
de la mujer obrera en Tijuana, B.C.N.* Mexico City: Cefnomex, 1985.
75–93.

James, Karen M., Jean M. Langdon, Thomas A. Langdon, Kerry J. Pa-
taki, Lynn D. Patterson and Steven S. Webster. "The Endless Cycle:
Migrant Life in the Yakima Valley." Diss. University of Washington,
1967.

Lafaye, Jacques. *Quetzalcóatl and Guadalupe: The Formation of Mexican National Consciousness, 1531–1813.* Trans. Benjamin Keen.
Chicago: University of Chicago Press, 1976.

Langewiesche, William. *Cutting for Sign: One Man's Journey along the
U.S.–Mexican Border.* New York: Vintage–Random, 1993.

León Portilla, Miguel. *El reverso de la Conquista: Relaciones Aztecas,
Mayas e Incas.* 1964. México City: Planeta, 1988.

Lopez Austin, Alfredo. *The Rabbit on the Face of the Moon: Mythology
in the Mesoamerican Tradition.* Trans. Bernard R. Ortiz de Montellano and Thelma Ortiz de Montellano. Salt Lake City: University of
Utah Press, 1996.

López Guido, Francisco. "Morelia de ayer y de siempre." *Urbanización
y Desarrollo en Michoacán.* Ed. Gustavo López Castro. Zamora: El
Colegio de Michoacán, 1991. 287–337.

Martinez, Rubén. *Crossing Over: A Mexican Family on the Migrant
Trail.* New York: Picador, 2002.

———. *The Other Side: Notes from the New L.A., Mexico City, and
Beyond.* New York: Vintage-Random, 1992.

Massey, Douglas, Rafael Alarcón, Jorge Durand and Humberto
González. *Return to Aztlán: The Social Process of International Mi-
gration from Western Mexico.* Studies in Demography 1. Berkeley:
University of California Press, 1990.

McDowell, John H. *Poetry and Violence: The Ballad Tradition of Mexico's Costa Chica.* Music in American Life, Folklore and Society 15.
Urbana: University of Illinois Press, 2000.

McKenna, Teresa. *Migrant Song: Politics and Process in Contemporary Chicano Literature*. Austin: University of Texas Press, 1997.

Meyer, Jean. *La Cristiada: Obra completa*. 2nd ed. 4 Vols. Mexico City: Clío, 1999.

Moheno, Roberto Blanco. *Cuando cardenas nos dio la tierra*. Barcelona: Bruguera, 1980.

Monsiváis, Carlos. *Los rituales del caos*. Mexico City: Biblioteca Era, 1995.

Ochoa Serrano, Alvaro. *La violencia en Michoacán: Ahi viene Chávez García*. Zamora: El Colegio de Michoacán, 1990.

Ochoa Serrano, Álvaro, ed. *Viajes de michoacanos al norte*. Zamora: El Colegio de Michoacán, 1998.

Pérez, Ramón (Tianguis). *Diary of an Undocumented Immigrant*. Translated by Dick J. Reavis. Houston, Tex.: Arte Publico Press, 1991.

Poppa, Terrence E. *Drug Lord: The Life and Death of a Mexican Kingpin*. Seattle, WA: Demand, 1998.

Preston, Julia and Samuel Dillon. *Opening Mexico: The Making of a Democracy*. New York: Ferrar, 2004.

Ramírez, Luis Alfonso. *Chilchota: un pueblo al pie de la Sierra: Integración regional y cambio económico en el noroeste de Michoacán*. Zamora: El Colegio de Michoacán, 1986.

Ramos Arizpe, Guillermo. *Relatos de don Jesús Ramos Romo: Narración e historia personal*. Jiquilpán, Mich.: Centro de Estudios de la Revolución Mexicana, 1986.

———. "Testimonio de trabajadores michoacanos en Estados Unidos en los años vientes 1920–1930." *Boletín del Centro de Estudios de la Revolucion Mexicana* June 1983: 35–74.

Relaciones Geográficas of Mexico and Guatemala, 1577-1585. Benson Latin American Collection, General Libraries, University of Texas at Austin.

Rionda Ramírez, Luis Miguel. *Y jalaron pa'l norte . . . : Migración, agrarismo y agricultura en un pueblo Michoacano: Copándaro de Jiménez*. Mexico: Instituto Nacional de Antropología e Historia, 1992.

Rotella, Sebastian. *Twilight on the Line: Underworlds and Politics at the U.S.–Mexico Border*. New York: Norton, 1998.

Shorris, Earl. *Latinos: A Biography of the People*. New York: Avon, 1992.

Tavera Alfaro, Xavier. "Morelia la nunca bien ponderada." *Urbanización y Desarrollo en Michoacán*. Ed. Gustavo López Castro. Zamora: El. Colegio de Michoacán, 1991. 213–32.

Taylor, Lawrence J. *Tunnel Kids*. Photos by Maeve Hickey. Tucson: University of Arizona Press, 2001.

Turner, Kay F. *Niño Fidencio: A Heart Thrown Open*. Photographs and Interviews by Dore Gardner. Santa Fe: Museum of New Mexico Press, 1992.

Urrea, Luis Alberto. *Across the Wire: Life and Hard Times on the Mexican Border*. New York: Anchor, 1993.

———. *By the Lake of Sleeping Children: The Secret Life of the Mexican Border*. New York: Anchor–Doubleday, 1996.

Valle, Isabel. *Fields of Toil: A Migrant Family's Journey*. Pullman: Washington State University Press, 1994.

Vázquez León, Luis. "La Meseta Tarasca: Los municipios 'indigenas.'" *Estudios Michoacanos I*. Ed. Carlos Herrejón Peredo. Zamora: El Colegio de Michoacán, 1986. 75–93.

"Vecinos—Neighbors: [a special series on Michoacan, Mexico and Mexican farm workers in Yakima]." *Yakima Herald-Republic*, February 26–March 5, 1995.

Wald, Elija. *Narcocorrido: A Journey into the Music of Drugs, Guns, and Guerrillas*. New York: Reyo, 2001.

ABOUT THE AUTHOR

Philip Garrison is the author of two previous nonfiction collections. *Augury* (University of Georgia Press, 1991) was selected by Robert Atwan as winner of the 1990 Associated Writing Programs Award for Creative Nonfiction, and received a Washington State governor's award for literary excellence. *Waiting for the Earth to Turn Over* (University of Utah Press) appeared in 1996.

He studied at the Universities of Missouri and Iowa. Since the early 1970s, he has rotated university teaching assignments between the Mexican Central Plateau and the U.S. Inland Northwest. In 1991 he held a Fulbright Fellowship to Central America.

With two friends, in 1995, he founded APOYO, a volunteer group that offers advocacy, interpretation services, and a food/clothing bank that now serves some 400 people a month from central Washington's mexicano communities.